GROWTH GAMES FOR THE CREATIVE MANAGER

Also by
Eugene Raudsepp

Creative Growth Games
More Creative Growth Games
How to Sell New Ideas
How Creative Are You?

GROWTH GAMES FOR THE CREATIVE MANAGER

Eugene Raudsepp

A PERIGEE BOOK

ACKNOWLEDGMENTS

It would be difficult to acknowledge individually all the people to whom I am indebted for encouragement, suggestions, ideas, and examples. Of particular relevance have been the seminal works and insights of J. P. Guilford, Ross L. Mooney, William J. J. Gordon, Donald W. MacKinnon, and Sidney J. Parnes.

I am most especially indebted to Arthur B. VanGundy, Sidney X. Shore, Joseph C. Yeager, and Ronald F. Becker who permitted me to use some of their exercises in my games and inventories. And I also want to express my appreciation to my daughter Kira for her perceptive suggestions, and her help in the organization and typing of the manuscript.

Perigee Books
are published by
The Putnam Publishing Group
200 Madison Avenue
New York, NY 10016

Typeset by Fisher Composition, Inc.

Library of Congress Cataloging-in-Publication Data

Raudsepp, Eugene.
    Growth games for the creative manager.

    "A Perigee book."
    1. Creative ability in business.   I. Title.
HD53.R359 1986   658.4'09   86-11267
ISBN 0-399-51281-0

Printed in the United States of America
1 2 3 4 5 6 7 8 9 10

Contents

Introduction   7
Profile of the Creative Manager   13

Games and Inventories   33

  1. Test Your Creativity Quotient   33
  2. Your Creative Achievements   36
  3. Insights into Self   37
  4. Crystallizing Your Values and
      Increasing Self-Understanding   39
  5. Building Your Skills Profile   49
  6. The Possible Dream   55
  7. Visualizing Your Goals   56
  8. Fear of Failure   59
  9. Other Uses   62
10. Verbal Dexterity I   62
11. Peripatetic Women   65
12. Suggestion Systems   65
13. Like/Unlike   66

14. What Could It Be?   68
15. Odd One Out   69
16. Are You Intuitive?   70
17. Taking Charge of Your Time   71
18. Are You Under the Right Amount of Stress?   74
19. Match Point   79
20. Coping with Neophobia   81
21. Smugnosis   81
22. Decisions, Decisions   82
23. Who's in Charge Here?   84
24. Test Your Work Pattern   86
25. Do You Fear Success?   89
26. Letters Will Do   91
27. What Does It Mean?   92
28. Who Owns the Zebra?   94
29. Nitty-Gritty   95
30. Stretching Perspectives   96
31. Linear Perspectives   97
32. S(i)MILE When You Say That   98
33. Clustering Ideas   99
34. What If?   100
35. Verbal Dexterity II   101
36. Sticky Fingers   103
37. How Well Do You Listen?   106
38. Overcoming Managerial Isolation   110
39. Strictly for the Birds   111
40. Problem Situations   113
41. Blocks and Barriers   114
42. Managing Creative People   115
43. Teamwork Dynamics   115
44. Closed/Open Systems   116
45. How to Evaluate Ideas   120
46. The Politics of Selling Ideas   121
47. Implementation   123
48. Innoways   124
49. 20/10 Vision   124
50. Never Reject an Idea . . .   125

Answers, Possibilities and Analyses   127

INTRODUCTION

Almost any modern business requires a continuous, unceasing flow of innovation in order to compete and to prosper. Creativity is needed to increase efficiency and productivity, to design and implement more economical and effective operating procedures, to improve the quality of products and services, and to tackle the increasingly stubborn and costly problems that rapid changes present. Creativity is needed to develop entirely new products and processes, to launch effective marketing strategies and sales campaigns, and to respond to new situations and challenges in an innovative way. A business organization which is not interested in innovation will not stay viable in the modern business world for long.

In analyzing the dynamics of past growth, more perceptive managements have made some revealing discoveries about the role that innovation has played in corporate success. Some corporations have estimated that as much as 90 percent of their sales volume comes from products unknown to the market a decade ago. And even more impressive is the fact that more than 45 percent of the entire gross national product has been attributed to creative research and development within the past fifteen years.

Creativity plays a fundamental role in thinking, problem solving, and decision making in almost all corporate functions. It is essential to management, planning, communications, marketing, advertising, sales, public relations, finance, labor relations, employee relations, recruiting, office automation, computer software, operations research, design, and so on. As experience has amply shown, creative problem-solving techniques can be applied to any and all business situations.

WHAT MAKES A CREATIVE COMPANY?

What do successful, creative companies have in common? Their one common denominator is that the tried, the proven, and the established do not have an inordinately strong hold on them. Instead of blindly following the dictates of established procedures, instead of prudent plodding, creative managers are willing to consider and utilize new creative ideas—even where the element of risk is considerable.

Creative managers are ever alert to new techniques and methods. They are ready to undertake pilot ventures. They are hospitable to new ideas and pioneering concepts which, because of their experimental nature, do not find ready acceptance in overly cautious companies, or in those companies where security is derived from the already consolidated success. Creative managers feel that they *can* afford to take chances, and *make* leaps into the unknown. They know that such action, even at the risk of many "dry wells" in the beginning, frequently delivers a real "gusher" in the end.

CREATIVITY AND ACCELERATING CHANGE

A business grows because it is constantly fed with new ideas. While effective use of ideas is valuable in good and stable times, it becomes absolutely essential in uncertain times, in times of changing values, shifting objectives, and new questions. In our ever more complex world it is no longer possible to rely solely on time-tested techniques and rational analysis to solve problems and to make the right decisions. Too many of the accepted and established techniques no longer serve adequately in coping with the new problems we face and *adequate* solutions to changing problems are no longer enough for a business to stay competitive.

Creativity is not only the name of the game in coping with and adapting to change; it is one of the most useful competitive tools for bringing constructive change about. In an enlightened business setup, it occupies the center stage.

THE PRESENT CLIMATE FOR CREATIVITY

Most business organizations are not doing enough to encourage innovation. Entrenched procedures remain in operation in spite of the need for change.

Of late, there has been much talk in news media and at conferences about the value of innovation. Most of it, unfortunately, only serves public and employee relations needs, and is a toothless expression of corporate attitudes.

The fact of the matter is that the present climate for innovation in most business organizations is rarely favorable. Most commonly it ranges from apathetic to passively or actively hostile. And such attitudes often pit the creative people and the people who have decision powers against one another.

To be sure, most business managers sincerely declare: "My door is always open to the person with a good idea." Experience, however, has shown that this policy is rarely enforced. The manager who tells a subordinate, "That is a good idea! Bring it back after you've worked out the details," may be delivering a death blow. Often the subordinate simply does not have the time, backing, incentive, or other resources necessary to continue the idea's development. Rare, indeed, is the manager who would devote the necessary effort toward helping the idea originator to amplify, clarify, and develop a convincing presentation or a demonstration that would awaken interest, defer negative judgment, and gain acceptance by top management.

In most businesses a real appreciation of the value of creativity, a sympathetic willingness to listen to and support new ideas, are lacking. Rare is the idea person who is sent away in a frame of mind to try again. Many seem to give up any further attempts to offer ideas, exclaiming, "He (or she) doesn't listen to me; he simply can't understand!" Others slip back into a more comfortable, and unproductive, conformity.

Reacting to low morale and the demands for a better quality

9

of work life, several organizations have come up with assorted palliative measures, such as sick and tired leaves, floating holidays, sanity breaks, playing hookey time, six-week sabbaticals every four years, 4 P.M. beer busts every Friday, and so on. These gimmicky measures might temporarily relieve excessive stress, but they do woefully little to increase creativity.

ROADBLOCKS TO CREATIVITY

To understand better why creativity fares so poorly in business, we have to consider the various roadblocks that exist. The pathways of most new ideas are blocked by:

- Resistance to change.
- Premature and uninformed judgments.
- Neophobia—the dread of anything new or novel; fear of the unknown.
- Sense of embarrassment or humiliation which accompanies the admission that existing products or procedures are inferior to new proposals.
- Caution. It's safer to have the "me-too-later" attitude.
- Threat to predictability and continuity on which all businesses are based. A new idea frequently represents a potential or real disruption of this continuity. The unwritten principle in business requires that disruptions be strictly controlled, or held to a minimum, no matter what they are.
- Anticipation of the extra trouble in handling and implementing new ideas. "We have enough work as is."
- Politics. New ideas frequently pose a threat to the organizational stature and vested interests of managers who are anxious to maintain the existing hierarchical structures.

Creative adaptation and flexibility represent the only viable alternative to business failure or stagnation. Educator David Mars put it well when he said, "Organizations which are creative and adaptive can view the future with the confidence that they will be able to cope with it; organizations which are not creative and adaptive will probably not see the changes coming in the first place, and when these changes arrive, will be overwhelmed by the stresses which they will create."

10

The purpose of this book is to provide: (1) A thorough grasp of the attributes and characteristics of the creative manager, (2) creative exercises and games to develop and bring to full flower one's latent creative potential, and (3) an understanding of what can be done to establish a creative climate.

Profile of the Creative Manager explores and explains the most vital characteristics of high-level creative functioning. *Games and Inventories* provides fifty exercises designed to release and develop a manager's creative powers. It is a comprehensive training program to enable you to: (1) Discover and utilize new facets of your imaginative and inventive powers to help you solve even the most difficult organizational problems; (2) Develop an understanding and insight into your behavior and thinking. *Guidelines for Establishing a Creative Climate* offers 97 strategies managers can use to establish a creative climate. It pinpoints the essential aspects of how to utilize, motivate, and manage individuals for enhanced creativity, and offers insights into the environmental and psychological conditions that best match the inherent requirements of creative functioning.

In the area of creativity and innovation even a small increase in efficiency can enormously expand the output and utilization of new ideas. If this book provides the needed techniques and exercises to accomplish this, its purpose will be amply rewarded.

Eugene Raudsepp
President
Princeton Creative Research, Inc.
Princeton, N.J.

PROFILE OF THE CREATIVE MANAGER

Even though there is obviously no single mold into which all creative managers fit, there are some distinct personality patterns and cognitive skills by which they can be identified and that significantly differentiate them from those managers who are less creative or even noncreative.

Before describing the creative managers' attributes in detail, it should be pointed out that no one manager could hope to possess all of these qualities to the same high degree. Rather, the descriptions should be taken as a composite profile of an "ideal." There are many gradations in the attributes and skills creative managers possess. However, every creative manager has at least some measure of these qualities in order to earn the appellation "creative." Certain combinations of personality traits frequently compensate for those attributes that are less developed, or have fallen into disuse.

It should also be pointed out that creativity is heavily dependent on the climate or culture of organizations. If the climate is inhospitable to the exercise of creative abilities, they will wither. Creative skills must be practiced and developed to be acquired in the first place, and continually used if they are to be increased or even retained. It has long been recognized that unpracticed skills "decay." In order to continue to be creative, a person must be allowed and encouraged to continually express his or her creative capacities.

Another thing that must be pointed out is that no attempt is made in this chapter to divide or classify these attributes into the customary cognitive, affective, and conative groupings. The reason for this is that the attributes of creativity are not self-contained units, but they overlap and merge into one another. It would be idle and meaningless to attempt to draw sharp lines between them. It is only to facilitate analysis and description that the characteristics are treated here as discrete entities.

What is the value of gaining insight into the attributes of the creative manager? Since people often learn by imitation, a manager can substantially increase his creative capacities and performance by deliberately cultivating those characteristics it is felt he does not possess to a sufficient degree or by "dusting off" those that have fallen into disuse. The reader would be well advised to study these characteristics closely, so they can become part and parcel of his personality makeup.

SELF-ESTEEM AND SELF-CONFIDENCE

A manager's self-image is crucial to his or her creative achievements because what he believes is possible for him directly influences his plans and actions. A manager who is convinced that he has attained his creative limits will cease to strive further. In contrast, a manager who believes that he can continue to reach for more challenging personal and organizational goals will keep on trying.

The creative manager constantly challenges his beliefs about his weaknesses and limitations. His self-esteem is secure and he does not have to constantly evade potential threats to it, nor does he feel a need to distort or deny experiences that might harm it.

In contrast, many less creative managers waste a lot of energy in maintaining and defending a good self-image. One strategy that is often used is to evade realities that threaten their idea of themselves and to filter out information that is offensive to their self-image. What remains is unrealistic and distorted.

Such a face-saving process impedes progress in self-knowledge.

14

It locks a manager into a rigid and idealized view of himself, causing him to blot out a full range of information that, if taken into account, would help to correct his shortcomings.

The creative manager is content to be the type of person he is. As a result, he has a healthy feeling that he can cope with problems, master challenges, and overcome obstacles. While he may occasionally experience brief periods of doubt about the outcome of his plans or projects, he seldom sees himself as being seriously limited in what he can do.

Every new creative accomplishment adds to the creative manager's feeling of self-confidence, and every new peak he reaches opens up new challenges. When serious setbacks and disappointments occur, he has the strength to survive them, because he never loses confidence in his powers and abilities. He believes in himself and is not devastated by a run of bad circumstances that are beyond his control.

FREEDOM FROM FEAR OF FAILURE

Because the career orientation of most managers is governed by the premise of success, the specter of failure looms large. In the risk-taking enterprise of innovation, however, failures sometimes do occur. No new ground anyone really wants to discover is completely secure under foot. One needs to respond positively to the risk and challenge of exploring new frontiers. As scientist James H. Austin puts it: "Creativity involves taking one step after another into pitch darkness—not a fussy rearranging of familiar furniture in a flood lighted room." The attitude that is requisite for risk-taking is also well expressed by the American painter, Albert Pinkham Ryder: "Have you ever seen an inchworm crawl up a leaf or twig and there, clinging to the very end, revolve in the air feeling for something to reach? That's like me. I'm trying to find something out there beyond the place I have a footing."

Fear of failure prevents many managers from daring anything really innovative, especially when it involves taking some risks. Their attitude of caution is dictated by their fear of the consequences of failure. Their valuable asset of being able to exercise sound judgment nevertheless qualifies their willingness to risk the kind of leap into the unknown that is almost always involved in genuine creative advances.

Actually, failure should be regarded as a "learning situa-

15

tion"—a situation from which new or improved ideas arise. Almost every area of business innovation has had its history of failures that ultimately led to success. In reality, the greatest failure is not to attempt a new idea at all. It would be well to heed Chester Barnard's sage advice: "To try and fail is at least to learn, to fail to try is to suffer the inestimable loss of what might have been."

HEALTHY SUCCESS ORIENTATION

Many managers are ambivalent about success—they *want*, but also want *not*, to succeed. Many have a subconscious wish to sabotage their projects just as they are on the brink of success. The high-powered creative manager is apparently free of this ambivalence—there are no ifs and buts about succeeding.

Success-guilt is a fairly common phenomenon, and it not only impedes many managers' career progress, but makes them feel unworthy of their accomplishments. The creative managers, in contradistinction, are not afflicted with a sense of guilt when they achieve ever higher creative goals.

There are basically ten reasons why creative managers are able to live a guilt-free existence: (1) They believe in what they are doing and are not compromising their basic values for increased status or money. Their creative successes are meaningful because they meet the standards of their own internal rods. (2) Their expectations do not outreach their creative accomplishments. Guilt often is a form of self-disappointment. It happens when a manager feels he has fallen short and somehow betrayed some internal sense of potential. (3) Their work fulfills the broader goals they want to achieve in their lives. (4) They are able to enjoy their creative accomplishments in a realistic way. (5) While critical of their own work, they are never supercritical and thus do not make things harder for themselves than is necessary. (6) They are honest with themselves and they appreciate their own strong points. They never play down their creative abilities or efforts. (7) They feel that success is a natural and healthy ambition, not a dirty word. (8) Their self-image meshes well with their outward success and they are free of subconscious conflicts about their goals. (9) They know how to balance loyalty to others with loyalty to themselves. (10) They believe that their creative endeavors make a valuable contribution to society.

CONSTRUCTIVE NONCONFORMITY

The creative manager knows how to make adjustments in his life without compromising his individuality. He can cope with the demands of his environment with minimal feelings of distress. Frequently he insists on designing and shaping his own environment, rather than be shaped by the milieu he happens to occupy. This is because his own private values and standards carry far more weight than those of his environment.

While the creative manager has a great need for independence and for calling his own shots, he does not make a show of his independence. He is not deliberately nonconformist, but genuinely autonomous. Because he displays assertive self-assurance and is not easily influenced by the opinions around him, he may appear insensitive to the attitudes and feelings of others. But his driving single-mindedness in the pursuit of his objectives is essential, for without it he would lack the perseverance to develop his ideas into something viable. Most organizations have managers who produce excellent ideas, but they lack the courage to be their own person, to overcome opposition, and to turn their ideas into concrete, living products.

Many less creative managers adjust to their environments at a considerable cost. They confine their actions to narrow, prescribed limits, and try to fit neatly into all situations. Because they tend to unquestioningly accept the dictates of the system, they feel that it might be superfluous and somewhat dangerous to rock the boat with new ideas. Their form of adjustment, motivated as it is by the desire to belong, to be accepted, and to win approval, is a form of self-betrayal: a denial of their preferences, values, and goals.

Even when such managers have a wide range of choices they could act upon, they are unable to summon guidance from themselves because they essentially distrust their own thoughts and feelings. At times they might sense a conflict between their real needs and what their conformity-conditioned personality dictates they ought to do. They are apt to resolve this conflict by bypassing their true selves and by assuming the roles that are expected of them.

Most organizations, unfortunately, reward and reinforce conformity: there is a strong disapproval of questioning, intolerance of independence in judgment and thinking, disapproval of risk-taking, and preoccupation with busy-work. High rewards go to those who are willing to silently accept authority's dicta, who are courteous, who do their work on time, who are obedient and well liked by their peers. The fact of the matter is, however, that many of these conforming managers are rigid, stereotyped, uninsightful, and woefully lacking in spark or drive.

COURAGE AND OPTIMISM

Creative managers have the courage to live with ambiguity, incompleteness, uncertainties, complexity, doubts, mysteries, and perplexities without reaching immediately after facts and reason, or rushing to form judgments. Confusion does not make them anxious.

But most importantly, they are unafraid to pierce the barriers of the known and to penetrate into the expanse of the unknown, to take risks, to seize upon chance. The creative manager dauntlessly faces the risks that all new ventures carry and gives his projects his best.

The world is crowded with "just average" managers because their excessive dependency on others prevents them from going after what they want to accomplish. That the fear of others' opinions and judgments may constitute one of the most formidable barriers to innovative actions was pointed out by Ralph Waldo Emerson when he said, "Whatever you do, you need courage. Whatever course you decide upon, there is always someone to tell you you are wrong. There are always difficulties arising which tempt you to believe that your critics are right. To map out a course of action and follow it to an end, requires some of the same courage which a soldier needs."

Creative managers also have a basic, unassailable optimism that is vital for any inventive undertaking. Without the belief that what is being sought can be achieved, efforts will inevitably lag. Optimism is the underlying spirit that sustains creative managers when the outcome is not immediate, but somewhere in the future.

While optimism without action degenerates into mere wishful thinking, innovative action without optimism is impotent. Managers who lack optimism tend to trust their negative projections about possible outcomes more than they do their optimistic scenarios. Although optimism is sometimes hard to justify intellectually, it is nevertheless necessary to bring creative objectives—especially difficult ones—to fruition.

HEALTHY CONCERN

Worry is a form of fear. When worry becomes habitual, it forms a channel into which all thoughts are drained, producing discouragement and depression. By letting fear hold sway, a person imbues the atmosphere around him with uncertainty and doubt. This doubt often creates the conditions that lead to failure.

The creative manager has a healthy concern for problems, but he does not worry. There is a world of difference between the two attitudes. When a person is worried, he tries to escape from his problems. With an attitude of concern, a person strives to tackle and solve problems using his resources to bring about the outcome he seeks. As Mark Twain once said, "Worry is like a rocking chair. It goes back and forth, but gets you nowhere."

MODERATE RISK TAKING

Contrary to a popular stereotype that sees the creative manager as a gambling high risk-taker, effective managers have been found to prefer taking calculated risks in which the chances of winning are not so small as to be a sure thing, nor so large as to be a gamble. They set themselves goals that tend to be rather high and challenging, yet at the same time attainable. There are creative managers, of course, who prefer more formidable challenges. As one creative manager put it, "Since I was a little boy there was nothing I thought I couldn't do. I like to bite off more than I can supposedly chew, and then succeed." But most creative managers prefer to pitch their aspirations just a notch above the level of their own capabilities to provide them with a feeling of comfortable challenge. Maintaining an unrealistically high level of ambition not only makes failure possible, it also instills a fear of failure, which can be more damaging than the failure itself.

There are creative managers who aim high, knowing fully well that they might not quite attain their goal. They seem to be aware of an interesting "law" about aspiration: If you aim for only 25 percent of the possible, you are apt not to exceed it because this limit becomes fixed in your mind. If, on the other hand, you shoot for 100 percent, you may fall short of this mark, but the sheer intention of going for it all will place you far beyond the 25 percent point.

REALITY ORIENTATION

Creative managers are intellectually honest and ready to confront facts squarely when they are wrong. Most people have built-in filters that screen out the boos and amplify the applause. Not so the creative manager. He knows when he is in trouble, and has the ego-strength to admit when he is wrong.

Although it is probably impossible to rid oneself of all illusions about oneself, about others, and about the world, creative managers make it a point to clearly perceive and understand the various levels of reality, and they are willing to rid themselves of the more comforting or soothing of illusions. This reality orientation enables them to better determine what is and what is not possible to accomplish.

RESPONSIBILITY

Another important attribute of the creative manager is a belief that mistakes and setbacks are only temporary detours along the way to achieving a goal. Unlike some managers who get into a habit of retreat and withdrawal after suffering a defeat, he has the ability to recover rapidly from mistakes. He doesn't hide from his mistakes, nor does he dismiss them. He concedes that the mistakes have occurred and immediately proceeds to analyze what caused them. He wants to learn from them and use the knowledge to prevent future problems, rather than brushing the error off as someone else's fault or bad luck.

The creative manager also shows great flexibility in the way he handles mistakes. He may decide that, because his original plan was correct, he should expend whatever effort is needed to correct the mistakes; or he may conclude that the original plan had some serious flaws in it and should be dropped; or he may decide to look for an unrecognized opportunity in the mistakes. Such flexibility enables him to determine what he can or cannot accomplish at any point in time.

CHALLENGE AND CHANGE

Creative managers seldom experience any undue anxieties and fears in the face of change. And most of them not only know how to adapt to change, but insist on being proactive participants in the process, thus influencing the direction in which the changes are going to take place.

Many creative managers welcome the challenge of change. After having attained an important objective, they immediately set out to pursue another challenging goal. Because they like to conquer difficulties, they even manage to convert unforeseen problems into challenges.

Less creative managers, in contrast, view the challenge of change with timidity and trepidation. Changes represent a break in a predictable routine and pose a threat to their fragile sense of security. Lacking the creative manager's stress-resistant hardiness, they often wonder, "Who knows what will happen if I pursue this goal?" And frequently there is an inclination to fear the worst. Beset by doubts, they often start fighting their own goals even before they have had a chance to get started. Eventually they become motivationally flaccid and timorous, risking less and less. Their resistance restricts the number of changes they can make to improve their organizations. It prevents them from exploring new possibilities and alternative ways to enhance the profitability of their companies.

MOTIVATION

Preconditions to creative achievement in any field are a strong emotional commitment and a need to test one's limits. Most managers have a need to come up with novel and useful ideas, but in creative managers this need is uncommonly powerful. For an idea to grow into a viable, full-fledged product, it has to be tackled with visceral fervor.

The creative manager likes to involve himself in projects he finds deeply interesting and that in some way satisfy his deepest needs. To work at the intensity demanded by innovative work, the manager must find full satisfaction in the work itself, aside from any external satisfaction of potentially increased status, prestige, or money. He is governed more by inner stimulus than by outer accoutrements of success.

The highly creative manager is frequently haunted by his projects and he cannot let go of them. Anyone who has observed the creative manager at work has been impressed by the fully absorbed and vigorous concentration that infuses his activity. His strong sense of purpose and commitment to his tasks shows strong ego-involvement which allows him to access and mobilize his energy. He exhibits unusual staying power.

The creative manager goes to great lengths to find projects that are most inclusive of his interests and of real challenge to his capacities. His chosen work is the most important avenue for the fulfillment of his life.

CREATIVE EXCITEMENT

Excitement gives much more than mere spice to life. Without excitement and sustained zest, long-term creative effort cannot be maintained. Excitement is so central to creative ideation that creativity itself can be defined as a by-product of excitement: Whenever perception, thinking, or action is accompanied and powered by excitement, we are dealing with creativity.

If excitement plays such a large role in creativity, and most managers are certainly capable of this emotion, why aren't more managers creative? First, most managers are capable of creative perception, thought, and action. What makes certain managers appear unusually creative is their *continuous* pervasive interest and excitement in new challenges and problems. Just as an athlete enjoys more and more the exercise of his muscles, a creative manager learns to enjoy more and more the use of his creative faculties. To think and to create, a manager must feel committed, must feel excited and continually rewarded by concrete achievements. Creative competence cannot be achieved in the absence of a sustaining interest, and the development of creative competence is peculiarly vulnerable to lack of interest or excitement.

PROBLEM-SOLVING BEHAVIORS

The beginning stages of mapping out a creative strategy often require considerable attention to detail. Even before the creative manager makes an attempt to secure a beachhead, he proceeds to rehearse and test the logistics and tactics. With all his painstaking attention to detail, he is able to balance facts and deliberation with intuitive decision making.

In the end, the creative manager must strongly rely on his own hunches, and he trusts them. But at the same time he respects facts and pays attention to details. When problems occur, he knows by deduction and observation where the root causes lie, and he can focus for long periods on those important areas and exclude what is irrelevant. He is sensitive to continuous feedback on his performance and prefers to take immediate corrective action when things are not going according to plan.

Before they embark on a project, creative managers saturate themselves with details to facilitate the analysis of particular tasks that have to be performed. Immersion in details often acts to balance overheated imaginations.

DIVERGENT FLEXIBILITY AND ORIGINALITY

Most managers think convergently, seeking the one right answer to a problem as determined by the given facts. Creative managers, on the other hand, prefer to approach problems in a divergent manner, going off in different directions, seeking several possibilities rather than the one right answer. If new developments or changed circumstances demand it, they can easily drop one line of thought and pursue other conceptual possibilities. They constantly approach problems with "What else?" or "What would happen if I shifted perspectives and viewpoints?" They have no compulsive need to arrive at a premature closure, but prefer to consider many possible solutions.

In addition to, or perhaps because of, his flexibility, the creative manager is able to perceive previously unseen patterns and connections in problem situations and then solve them in an original fashion.

Since his thought processes are not jammed up with stereotypes, he can reach out beyond the commonplace and think of more unusual solutions to his problems. His originality expresses itself also in his ability to take apart firmly structured and established systems, to dissolve existing syntheses, and to use elements and concepts beyond the limits they possess in their primary contexts, to create a new system of relationships.

In addition to this faculty to fragment and differentiate, the creative manager is able to find unity and diversity, to see unexpected connections between experiences, and phenomena that evidence no relationship whatever to the less creative manager.

TOLERANCE OF AMBIGUITY

One significant reason for the lack of ability to produce creative ideas among some managers is their strong preference for the precise and tangible. As a result, they often tend to reject thoughts and ideas that do not fit into what they already know. Vagueness, or strangeness, is experienced as a scary, uncomfortable, and sometimes even an irresponsible state of mind by many managers. They find ambiguity threatening and prefer the tried-and-tested and immediately comprehensible patterns, thoughts, and situations. The familiar is secure and the new appears as a threat to their feelings of security.

The creative manager, on the other hand, is not afraid of ambiguity. On the contrary, he seems rather attracted to phenomena that are not readily comprehended, and he is drawn to complex situations. As a result, he is aware of, and open to, the intricate and paradoxical qualities of many situations. Like other managers, he seeks integration and order, but he is willing to seek it without prematurely shutting out his awareness of the chaotic or the ambiguous.

CURIOSITY AND PLAYFULNESS

Creativity is, in an important sense, contingent upon the preservation of sense of wonder and a heightened awareness of the world. The creative manager shows fresh, almost childlike awe of the external world, always ready to see something unexpected and unusual in all of his experiences. He retains his pristine sense of curiosity.

The creative manager's attitude of curiosity and wide-awake interest invariably extends far beyond the confines of his specialty or fields. His wide spectrum of interest includes many related and unrelated areas and he can get excited about almost any problem or phenomenon that puzzles him. Many things that are taken for granted by others are for him full of mystery and challenge. In this sense he is intellectually restless, not satisfied with what is accepted or established. He is constantly wondering how things could or might be, always ready to consider and visualize new possibilities. He feels that it is necessary to improve upon, or add to, existing things, and he refuses to accept the proposition that the last word has ever been said on the solution to any problem. It is said that necessity is the mother of invention, but there has been a curious lack of interest in discovering who the father is. Could it be that the father is curiosity?

There is also a seemingly light side to the creative manager's attitude toward new ideas. When he thinks of a fantastic or improbable idea, his first inclination is to mentally toy with its implications and possibilities, to see its value. Less creative managers tend to immediately dismiss or disapprove unusual ideas and show how impractical or infeasible they are.

The creative manager has learned from past experience that toying with ideas relaxes the critical bent of his consciousness. A lighthearted spirit of play frees him from the conditionings and conventions that impede the arrival of the new. By putting the judicial censor of his conscious mind to sleep, so to speak, he can transcend the established order and set the stage for the premiere of creative ideas.

PERSISTENCE AND CONCENTRATION

Some creative managers become so absorbed in their projects that for a period they pursue them with a single overriding purpose, shunting aside regular work, even neglecting their family obligations, and completely ignoring their daily schedules. The creative manager has a single-mindedness that helps him to persist in the face of repeated disappointments and occasionally even intense frustration. Although he sometimes experiences failure, he is not crushed by it, but feels the experience is only temporary and will exhaust itself if he continues to stay the course regardless of the obstacles.

Creation is preceded by hard thinking and total absorption. There is a continuous assimilation of new knowledge and experience, a continuous pondering on the causes of the difficulties that are met and a sorting out of ideas that flash across the conscious. It is apparent that all this takes time and willingness to experience and accept many agonies.

Quite often the conscious efforts are abortive and useless in the beginning stages of creative problem solving. Creative managers have testified that many times they had to temporarily give up their efforts, and that many of their initial attempts ended in failure before a valid solution or idea emerged. Still, all these apparently futile initial efforts are not as wasted as they seem. They serve the function of activating the subconscious processes of cerebration and incubation. Without preparatory work, the subconscious can be notoriously unproductive.

It is true that some creative managers rely more deliberately on the gestative process of the subconscious to complete the ideas for them. With most creative managers, however, intense preliminary effort and a lot of exhausting spadework constitutes the necessary prelude to original production. The capacity for original work grows out of diligence and unflagging persistence.

Discomfort with persistence or a feeling of fading interest is often a signal for the need to get away from a problem and to relax for awhile. Creative managers often find that they can relax by working on another challenging project. Many of them say that they function best when involved in several undertakings simultaneously, each at a different stage of development, each affording an opportunity to relax when the ability to persist with one particular project falters.

Persistence is required in testing and polishing the project so that the many minuses are eliminated. Further persistence is needed in selling others on the merits of the idea and putting it into practice. Finely honed political and people-oriented skills are required because a novel product in most organizations cannot survive until the support of other people is secured.

There comes a time during creative problem solving when thinking gets ponderous or clogged, when errors start to pile up and no further developments occur. This is the time when the creative manager ceases his work on the problem and turns to some other project. Many creative managers find a welcome change of pace in music, painting, sightseeing, manual tasks, daydreaming, reverie, etc. These activities provide a refreshing interlude and allow the subconscious mental activities the freedom to operate unrestrained by conscious concentration.

Although the creative manager spends a great deal of his conscious effort to solve a problem, he realizes the limitations of this effort and finally resorts to incubation. As psychologist John M. Schlien points out: "Although he has confidence in his ability, the creative person also has an attitude of respect for the problem and admits the limits of his conscious power in forcing the problem to solution. At some point, called 'incubation' by many who have reported the process, he treats the problem 'as if it had a life of its own,' which will, in its time and in its relation to his subliminal or autonomous thought processes, come to solution. He will consciously work on the problem, but there comes a point when he will sleep on it." The subconscious autonomous thought processes take over during the incubation period and continue solving the problem. Frequently, while the conscious forcing of the problem to solution failed, the incubatory process succeeds.

The creative manager schedules his creative thinking periods for those times when he has his most favorable mental set for producing ideas. He is aware of his personal rhythms and peaks and valleys of output. By keeping a record of those periods during the day or night in which he is most creative, he can establish a pattern and plan ahead, reserving the peak periods for problem solving and uninhibited thinking. Even if he has not established a time sheet of creative periods, he has at least developed a sensitivity to those moods that promise creative returns from his efforts, and he knows when they are approaching.

AESTHETIC ORIENTATION

Highly creative individuals in all fields have been noted for their strong aesthetic sensitivities and their love of the arts. This observation, gleaned from biographies, remained rather incidental and anecdotal until it was experimentally proven by a group of behavioral scientists at the Institute of Personality Assessment and Research in Berkeley, California. Here, in a comfortable, home-like atmosphere of a converted fraternity house, a group of psychologists engaged in one of the most intensive and thorough studies of the creative individual undertaken anywhere in the world.

The procedure, which they termed "the living-in method of assessment," entailed bringing to the Institute groups of highly creative individuals for a period of several days, during which time they were subjected to batteries of psychological tests, personality scales, in-depth interviews, and behavioral observations. Hundreds of creative individuals—architects, research scientists, inventors, business executives, engineers, mathematicians, artists, and writers—nominated by their peers as highly original persons in their respective fields, have been studied by this method.

One of the instruments the investigators used was the highly accepted *Study of Values Test* which measures the relative dominance of six basic interests and values: theoretical, economic, aesthetic, social, political, and religious. The classification is based on the works of the psychologist Eduard Spranger, who maintained that the personalities of people are best known by the values they hold. The significant finding with this test was that the creative subjects from widely diverse fields all scored highest on the "aesthetic" and "theoretical" scales, considerably higher than on the "political," "economic," "social," and "religious" scales.

Many creative managers claim that openness to the aesthetic sense enables them to arrive at a unique and dynamic integration of the images and thoughts they use. In addition, it permits them to function with the greatest economy of time, energy, and resources.

Several recent innovative seminars in the area of management development, problem solving, and decision making have made use of art-type experiences and activities—ranging from "painting a mess," doodling with colored pens, drawing human figures and landscapes, using modeling clay, and making block designs to interpreting films, listening to musical selections, and creating poems. The rather astounding results with these unorthodox methods, used on practical, profit-oriented managers and executives in the business world, are that they all report gains far surpassing those that are accomplished with the standard techniques used in management training. Even a few days' worth of art experiences lead them to increased sensitivity, enhanced problem solving capacity, efficiency, and a feeling of dynamic equilibrium and well-being.

OTHER CHARACTERISTICS

Here are some of the other characteristics which differentiate the more creative manager from the less creative:

· He is more observant and perceptive, and he puts a high value on independent insight. He perceives things the way other people do, but also the way others do not.

· He is more independent in his judgments. His self-directive behavior is determined by his own set of values and standards of judgment. He prefers to find things out for himself rather than accept them on authority.

· He balks at group standards, conformity pressures, and external controls. He asserts his independence without being hostile or aggressive and he speaks his mind without being domineering. If needs be, he is flexible enough to simulate the prevailing norms of organizational behavior.

· He dislikes policing himself and others; he does not like to be bossed around. He can readily entertain impulses and ideas that are commonly considered tabu, or that break with convention. He has a spirit of adventure.

· He is highly individualistic and nonconventional in a constructive manner. Psychologist Donald W. MacKinnon puts it this way: "Although independent in thought and action, the creative manager does not make a show of his independence; he does not do the offbeat thing narcissistically, that is, to call attention to himself. . . . He is not a deliberate nonconformist but a genuinely independent and autonomous person."

· He has a rich reservoir of knowledge and broad interests which span many seemingly unrelated fields. He has the interest and potential sufficient to succeed in several careers.

· He makes education and the acquisition of new knowledge a vital part of his career design. His goal is to become intellectually broad without spreading himself thin.

· His memory storage is rich of facts, observations, impressions, ideas, and associations which are cross-indexed. Such a permeable memory structure is open to the formation of new combinations of ideas.

· He is constitutionally energetic and, when creatively engaged, can marshal an exceptional fund of psychic and physical energy.

· He is less anxious and possesses greater stability.

· His complex personality has, simultaneously, more primitive and more cultured, more destructive and more constructive, crazier and saner aspects. He has a greater appreciation and acceptance of the nonrational elements in himself and others.

· He is open to inner feelings and emotions. This enables him to be spontaneous and uninhibited. It is easy for him to relate to others how he feels and what he thinks.

· He is willing to entertain and express personal impulses, and pays attention to his "inner voices." He likes to see himself as being different from others, and he has greater self-acceptance.

· He has strong aesthetic drive and sensitivity, and a greater interest in the artistic and aesthetic fields. He prefers to order the forms of his own experience aesthetically and the solutions he arrives at must not only be creative, but elegant.

· He searches for philosophical meanings and theoretical constructs and tends to prefer working with ideas, in contradistinction to the less creative managers who prefer to deal with the practical and concrete.

· He has a greater need for variety, and is almost insatiable for intellectual ordering and comprehension.

· He places great value on humor of the philosophical sort, and possesses a unique sense of humor.

· He regards authority as arbitrary, contingent on continued and demonstrable superiority. He separates source from content when evaluating communications. He reaches conclusions based on his judgment of the information itself, and not on whether the information source was an "authority."

· He is determined to finish a project once undertaken, even under conditions of frustration. He perseveres in his work despite obstacles or opposition.

· He insists on isolating himself from the distractions and interruptions of his environment in order to fully concentrate on the creative task at hand.

· He is a dynamic individual, irritated with the status quo, and he refuses to be restricted by habit and environment.

· He is able to open himself up to experiences and abandon defenses. He is honest with himself and able to examine himself and his ideas with objectivity.

· He is not self-satisfied or complacent.

· He is independent of others in his judgment. While he is willing to listen to suggestions and advice, he is determined to judge for himself.

· He does not blame others or make excuses for his own errors or failures.

· He is alert to new perspectives, knowing that so much depends on the angle from which something is grasped. When he gets stuck in problem solving, he knows that this is frequently due to the fact that he is asking the wrong questions.

· He has picturesque, vivid, and colorful imagery. He can form mental images of what is not actually present to the senses, or what he never has actually experienced. He is able to create new images by combining previously unrelated ideas.

· He has the ability to "look inside" his problems and to sense intuitively which elements are relevant and which are not. He is able to judge which factors must be taken into account in problem solving and which can be neglected or discarded without risk of error.

· He is governed by inner stimulus rather than by outer demand, and has a rising level of aspiration.

· He has a good grasp of general economic concepts.

· He is a mature, self-assured individual, able to interact well with people of varying personalities and values. He is able to exercise control over his impulses and feelings.

· He has the ability to make the very best of the resources at hand.

PARADOXICAL CHARACTERISTICS

Creative managers have been able to integrate into their personalities a number of apparent paradoxes. These are:

• A general nondefensive openness to the world around them that permits perception of the richness of everything with which they come into contact. At the same time they possess a stable organizing ability that provides them with a buffer to unpleasant surprises.

• A need to relate in harmony with others, but they also strive for independence, self-adequacy, and individual achievement. They are consultative, yet courageously independent.

• Inner locus of control and solid confidence, but they are also able to be self-critical and realistically appraise their limitations.

• An optimistic, confident stance toward life and the future. At the same time, however, they can be fully aware of any existing negative situations.

• Resourcefulness in tackling problems and making plans, but they are also prudent and circumspect; they are flexible, yet principled.

• Ability to analyze and reflect upon experiences, as they occur, but also the ability to act spontaneously, with no reflection.

Nondefensive openness is of particular importance in this list

31

of polarities. This permits the creative manager to learn from experiences, increase his total awareness, and undertake daring new actions. At the same time, however, the creative manager also exercises deliberate and systematic control over his actions when pursuing his goals. This disciplined mode favors stable progress and protection from unexpected events.

It should be noted that both of these modes occur in the creative process—there is an interplay of two distinct processes—the radically changing and the preservative, the diversifying and the unifying, the differentiating and the integrative.

GAMES AND INVENTORIES

1	Test Your Creativity Quotient*

How creative are you? The following test will help you to determine, through your personality traits, attitudes, values, motivations, and interests, how creatively you think. It is based on several years' study of attributes possessed by creative managers in a variety of fields and occupations.

For each statement write the appropriate letter in the blank:
A——Agree
B——Undecided or don't know
C——Disagree.

Be as frank as possible. Try not to guess how you feel a creative manager might respond.

---

*Answers and analyses to this and the following inventories and games begin on p. 127.

1. I always work with a great deal of certainty that I am following the correct procedure for solving a particular problem. _____
2. It would be a waste of time for me to ask questions if I have no hope of obtaining answers. _____
3. I concentrate harder on whatever interests me than most people do. _____
4. I feel that a logical step-by-step method is best for solving problems. _____
5. I occasionally voice opinions that seem to turn some people off. _____
6. I spend a great deal of time thinking about what others think of me. _____
7. It is more important for me to do what I believe to be right than to try to win the approval of others. _____
8. People who seem uncertain about things lose my respect. _____
9. More than other people, I need to have things that are interesting and exciting to work. _____
10. I know how to keep my inner impulses in check. _____
11. I am able to stick with different problems over extended periods of time. _____
12. On occasion I get overly enthusiastic. _____
13. I often get my best ideas when doing nothing in particular. _____
14. I rely on intuitive hunches and the feeling of "rightness" or "wrongness" when moving toward the solution of a problem. _____
15. I work faster when analyzing a problem and slower when synthesizing the information I have gathered. _____
16. I sometimes get a kick out of breaking the rules and doing things I am not supposed to do. _____
17. I like hobbies that involve collecting things. _____
18. Daydreaming has provided the impetus for many of my more important projects. _____
19. I like people who are objective and rational. _____
20. If I had to choose, I would rather be a physician than an explorer. _____
21. I can get along more easily with people if they belong to about the same social class and business level as myself. _____

34

22. I have a high degree of aesthetic sensitivity. _____
23. Status and power are important to me. _____
24. I like people who are confident in their conclusions. _____
25. Inspiration has nothing to do with the successful solution of problems. _____
26. When I am in an argument, I want the person who disagrees with me to like me, even at the price of sacrificing my point of view. _____
27. I am much more interested in coming up with new ideas than in trying to sell them to others. _____
28. I would enjoy spending an entire day alone, just thinking. _____
29. I tend to avoid situations in which I might feel inferior. _____
30. In evaluating information, the source is more important to me than the content. _____
31. I resent things being uncertain and unpredictable. _____
32. I like people who follow the rule, "business before pleasure." _____
33. Self-respect is much more important than the respect of others. _____
34. I feel that it is unwise to strive for perfection. _____
35. I prefer to work with others in a team effort rather than alone. _____
36. I like work in which I must influence others. _____
37. Many problems that I encounter cannot be resolved in terms of right or wrong solutions. _____
38. It is important for me to have a place for everything and everything in its place. _____
39. Writers who use strange and unusual words merely want to show off. _____
40. Below is a list of terms that describe people.

Choose 10 words that best characterize you.

___energetic	___factual	___courageous
___persuasive	___open-minded	___efficient
___observant	___tactful	___helpful
___fashionable	___inhibited	___perceptive
___self-confident	___enthusiastic	___quick
___persevering	___innovative	___good-natured
___original	___poised	___thorough

___cautious	___acquisitive	___impulsive
___habit-bound	___practical	___determined
___resourceful	___alert	___realistic
___egotistical	___curious	___modest
___independent	___organized	___involved
___stern	___unemotional	___absent-minded
___predictable	___clear-thinking	___flexible
___formal	___understanding	___sociable
___informal	___dynamic	___well-liked
___dedicated	___self-demanding	___restless
___forward-looking	___polished	___retiring

To determine and analyze your score, turn to page 128.

2 Your Creative Achievements

We all feel on occasion discouraged with a problem or project we're working on. The negative moods and mental attitudes we develop when no progress is made can sometimes persist for days or weeks. Fortunately, however, there is an exercise that can break the negative mind-set and set you free to attack your problem with vigor. It entails mentally reliving some successful achievements of the past—achievements you were proud of, enjoyed doing, and did well.

ON A SEPARATE PIECE OF PAPER BRIEFLY DESCRIBE THREE OF YOUR MAJOR ACHIEVEMENTS. WRITE DOWN WHAT WAS ACHIEVED, WHO WAS INVOLVED, WHEN YOU DID IT, WHY YOU DID IT, WHERE YOU DID, WHAT OBSTACLES YOU HAD TO OVERCOME, ETC. THESE ACHIEVEMENTS DON'T HAVE TO BE WORK-RELATED, BUT THEY SHOULD HAVE INVOLVED CONSIDERABLE CHALLENGE. NOW DECIDE WHICH IS THE MOST IMPORTANT ACHIEVEMENT TO YOU.

What you are aiming at here is to recapture the state of mind, the moods and feelings you had when you achieved something that meant a great deal to you. Try to recover the sense of confidence and energy you had when you realized that the achievement was within reach. Try to visualize and feel as clearly as you can all the details and circumstances of this achievement.

Now imagine that the problem or project you have to tackle will work out as well as everything did with your previous achievement. Cloak this mood of confidence and optimism around the problem you want to solve successfully.

Try also to imagine what the ideal outcome would be like, and how you would feel and act at the successful completion of the project. Try to hold on to this positive mood, this working frame of mind when you begin work on your present problem. Chances are that you will feel a tremendous surge of energy and find that you no longer have to force yourself to do the work. Your freed energy will push you along, and you will have the confidence and zeal to push forward.

<table>
<tr><td>3</td><td># Insights
into Self</td></tr>
</table>

To be a fully functioning creative manager you need to increase your self-knowledge and your awareness of your real needs, wishes, values, and the way you perceive your environment.

One of the most useful tools to accomplish this is the incomplete sentence exercise. It elicits a true, undistorted reaction that reveals your innermost feelings.

> ON A PIECE OF PAPER, WRITE THE FOLLOWING IN-
> COMPLETE SENTENCES, FINISHING EACH WITH THE
> FIRST SPONTANEOUS THOUGHT OR FEELING THAT
> OCCURS TO YOU.

To make sure you are tapping your truest and deepest feelings, try to complete this exercise in no more than three to four minutes.

1. To me, the future looks
2. I would like to
3. I can
4. I look forward to
5. Things would be better if
6. If I had the power
7. When the odds are against me
8. I get enough
9. Eventually, I'll be doing
10. I wish
11. My greatest mistake was
12. In the game of life, I
13. The best thing I ever did
14. I feel joy when
15. I always wanted to
16. I wish I could lose the fear of
17. Knowing the right people
18. I shall
19. I often enjoy
20. I believe I have the talent to
21. I spend much of my time
22. If I were young again
23. My dream is
24. I have always liked
25. I like people who
26. My best days are
27. I feel insulted when
28. Work is exciting when
29. One way to influence people is to
30. I look up to
31. I feel I am best at doing
32. My idea of a perfect life is
33. In a group I like to
34. I have accomplished
35. My greatest strength is
36. I trust those colleagues who
37. In a group I'm best at

38. I feel most productive when
39. Difference of opinion between
40. When I'm given an unusual assignment
41. When I make an important proposal
42. When conflict or tension arises
43. When I try to change something
44. The competition
45. When I need information, I
46. When a difference of opinion develops
47. When I have to make an important decision, I
48. When top management has problems
49. The attitude of my colleagues
50. Recognition

4 Crystallizing Your Values and Increasing Self-Understanding

An increasing number of managers these days are asking themselves the all-important questions: "What should I be doing to lead a full and successful life?", "Am I pursuing a career which is truly satisfying?" As these questions imply, managers have a strong need to get in touch with their futures.

It has been attested by one of our foremost psychologists, Carl R. Rogers, that self-discovery is the basis of psychological health and success. From treating thousands of patients he concludes that one central issue lies behind almost every problem—the lack of self-knowledge. In Rogers' therapeutic technique, success is recorded when the person begins to act more like his or her true self, dropping the masks and roles previously used. Only when a person begins to realize how much his actions have been based on mistaken notions of what he should be or what is expected of him, rather than on who he really is or wants to be, is he on the road to recovery.

According to research conducted by psychologist Stella Resnick, individuals who succeed in self-discovery are more capable of assuming self-responsibility. "Self-responsibility," she says, "means recognizing that you choose what you do and whom you are." When individuals take responsibility for their lives, they enlarge their alternatives and learn to make career choices that enhance and nourish them rather than deplete them.

One of the best ways to discover our true selves is to determine our values. Unfortunately, very few of us are fully aware of them at a conscious level. What is even worse, most of our values are not really our own, but have been imposed on us by parental upbringing, education, propaganda, and other outside pressures and standards.

So, the first thing to do is to define your values; then order them in terms of their importance. The following exercises will help you accomplish this with ease. Before you begin, remember the following points:

Clearly defined values will aid you in everything you do. In an important sense, your crystallized values serve as banisters on a staircase, to guide you, to be touched when you have to make decisions, and in very risky matters, grasped. There is always an element of risk in any form of decision making. The only way to reduce it is by studying the positive and negative implications of your choices in terms of their effect upon your value system. Then you can make a firm decision concerning the best alternative and accept whatever consequences may emerge.

When establishing your personal hierarchy of values, remember to be almost merciless in discarding those items you feel are no longer important. This way you will conserve energy for accomplishing the goals that mean most to you. Also, don't worry if some values seem equally desirable. Step back and evaluate them; chances are some will emerge much more important than others.

The first exercise will help you to prioritize your personal values. It will also show which of your values have already been satisfied, which are not important to you, and those value satisfactions you should try to increase.

Values Clarification
In the first (I) column, representing importance, assign a numerical value to each item as follows:

0–3 Low
4–6 Medium
7–10 High

In the second (S) column, representing satisfaction, assign a numerical value to each item as follows:

0–3 Very little or slightly
4–6 Moderately well
7–10 Fairly to extremely well

After you've finished marking the first two columns, pick out the scores you rated *high* in importance (I) and circle them; deduct the satisfaction (S) ratings from each of these and enter the values in the third (D) column, which represents your discrepancy scores.

	I	S	D
Accomplishment (achievement, fame, recognition, aspiration for excellence, lasting contribution)			
Aesthetics (appreciation of beauty, art, music)			
Affection (love, caring, becoming close and intimate with another person, being sensitive to the feelings of another person)			
Appearance (physical attractiveness, sex appeal)			
Autonomy (independence, self-direction, freedom, planning and directing own future)			
Competition (winning, being #1, liking competitive activity)			
Cooperation (participating with others, involvement)			
Creativity (using imagination, being innovative, problem-solving abilities)			
Devotion (strong spiritual beliefs, faith, transcending self through universal identification)			

	I	S	D
Economic security (comfortable life, freedom from economic worry)			
Emotional well-being (peace of mind, contentment, celebrating life, adapting to change, freedom from inner conflicts)			
Excitement (adventure, new experiences, challenge, risking, exploring, being enthusiastic)			
Expertness (being considered an authority)			
Family well-being (taking care of loved ones)			
Friendship (having close friends, companionship)			
Health (physical well-being)			
Helping others (humanitarianism, serving and working with others, concern for others, assuming community and social responsibility)			
Honesty (being sincere, open with others, integrity, courtesy)			
Intellectual (using your mind, liking to think, acquiring knowledge, studying)			
Leadership (influence, power, or control over others, being persuasive)			
Loyalty (sense of duty, trustworthiness)			
Money (wealth, getting rich)			
Personal growth (development, use of potential, self-realization)			
Play (pleasure, fun, leisurely life)			
Prestige (visible success, social recognition)			
Promotions (career advancement)			

	I	S	D
Recognition (status, respect from others, admiration)			
Responsibility (accountability, reliability, dependability)			
Self-acceptance (accepting one's strengths and limitations)			
Self-confidence			
Self-control (ability to control and inhibit undesirable behaviors, self-discipline)			
Self-respect (pride in self, self-esteem, strong sense of personal identity, having faith in talents and abilities)			
Stability (order, predictability, tranquillity)			

To analyze your discrepancy scores, see page 132.

Self-rating

This exercise will increase your self-understanding and indicate how you rate yourself on various important positive and negative characteristics, attitudes, and behaviors. Consider the extent to which you feel you possess each quality (very low, low, moderate, etc.) and place the appropriate symbol in column 1:

VL—Very low
L—Low
M—Moderate
H—High
VH—Very high

Place a D in column 2 if you would like to develop the characteristic, an M if you would like to minimize it.

If you are satisfied with the attribute—whether you checked it very low, low, high, etc.—place a check in column 3.

Characteristics	1	2	3
Ability to express thoughts	___	___	___
Ability to listen empathetically	___	___	___
Ability to work under pressure	___	___	___
Acquisitiveness	___	___	___
Adaptability	___	___	___
Aggressiveness	___	___	___
Ambition	___	___	___
Analytical ability	___	___	___
Anxiety	___	___	___
Arrogance	___	___	___
Aspiration for excellence	___	___	___
Assertiveness	___	___	___
Boredom	___	___	___
Cautiousness	___	___	___
Cheerfulness	___	___	___
Communication skills	___	___	___
Conceit	___	___	___
Concern for others	___	___	___
Conformity	___	___	___
Conscientiousness	___	___	___
Cooperativeness	___	___	___
Courage	___	___	___
Courteousness	___	___	___
Creativity	___	___	___
Cynicism	___	___	___
Decision-making ability	___	___	___
Dependability	___	___	___
Depression	___	___	___
Determination	___	___	___
Diplomacy	___	___	___
Distrust	___	___	___
Drive	___	___	___
Endurance	___	___	___
Energy level	___	___	___
Enthusiasm	___	___	___
Envy	___	___	___
Execution (follow-through)	___	___	___
Exhibitionism	___	___	___
Extraversion	___	___	___
Forcefulness	___	___	___

Characteristics	1	2	3
Friendliness	___	___	___
Frustration tolerance	___	___	___
Future orientation	___	___	___
Guilt	___	___	___
Honesty	___	___	___
Humility	___	___	___
Imagination	___	___	___
Impersonality	___	___	___
Impulsiveness	___	___	___
Independence	___	___	___
Indolence	___	___	___
Industriousness	___	___	___
Ingenuity	___	___	___
Initiative	___	___	___
Integrity	___	___	___
Interest in job	___	___	___
Intolerance	___	___	___
Introspectiveness	___	___	___
Introversion	___	___	___
Logic	___	___	___
Memory	___	___	___
Methodicalness	___	___	___
Moodiness	___	___	___
Nervousness	___	___	___
Orderliness	___	___	___
Organizing ability	___	___	___
Patience	___	___	___
Perfectionism	___	___	___
Persistence	___	___	___
Persuasiveness	___	___	___
Planning ability	___	___	___
Poise	___	___	___
Positive attitude	___	___	___
Procrastination	___	___	___
Professional ambition	___	___	___
Receptiveness	___	___	___
Resentment	___	___	___
Resourcefulness	___	___	___
Risk taking	___	___	___
Self-centeredness	___	___	___

Characteristics	1	2	3
Self-confidence	___	___	___
Self-discipline	___	___	___
Self-motivation	___	___	___
Self-pity	___	___	___
Self-understanding	___	___	___
Sense of humor	___	___	___
Sensitivity to people	___	___	___
Serious-mindedness	___	___	___
Sincerity	___	___	___
Snobbishness	___	___	___
Sociability	___	___	___
Social intelligence	___	___	___
Stubbornness	___	___	___
Submissiveness	___	___	___
Sullenness	___	___	___
Synthesizing ability	___	___	___
Tactfulness	___	___	___
Talkativeness	___	___	___
Time management	___	___	___
Tolerance for complexity	___	___	___
Tolerance for intangibles	___	___	___
Understanding of people	___	___	___
Variety	___	___	___
Worry	___	___	___

Personality Needs

Mark your answers to the following questions according to the key:

> **7–9** Strongly agree
> **4–6** Agree
> **1–3** Disagree

1. I like to accomplish difficult tasks. ___
2. I enjoy persuading and influencing people. ___
3. I don't mind telling people off when they deserve it. ___
4. At parties, I do most of the talking. ___
5. I prefer doing things with friends rather than alone. ___
6. I readily accept the leadership of others. ___
7. It is important for me to organize plans well. ___
8. I often seek encouragement from others. ___

9. It is important to be loyal to friends. _____
10. I like to let others make decisions. _____
11. I tend to persevere at a job until it is finished. _____
12. When I'm in trouble, I look for others to help me. _____
13. It is important to do a difficult job well. _____
14. I like to make group decisions. _____
15. I tend to be angry rather often. _____
16. I like to be the center of attention. _____
17. One should always do one's best. _____
18. I enjoy supervising and directing others. _____
19. I look for ways to get revenge for insults. _____
20. When I speak, I tend to use unusual words and expressions. _____
21. It is important for me to receive affection from others. _____
22. I need to work according to a system. _____
23. It is important for me to find out what others think. _____
24. I like to do things for friends. _____
25. I like telling amusing jokes and stories. _____
26. I often tell others what I think of them. _____
27. I enjoy being a leader in a group. _____
28. It is important for me to do things better than others. _____
29. I need to feel free of emotional and economic threat. _____
30. I always make advance plans. _____
31. I need to seek suggestions from others. _____
32. I like to have lots and lots of friends. _____
33. I like to be recognized as an authority. _____
34. I tend to argue my point of view. _____
35. I don't mind making fun of others. _____
36. I enjoy saying witty and clever things. _____
37. When I'm depressed or anxious, I like to be helped by others. _____
38. It is important for me to have things running smoothly. _____
39. I don't mind following instructions and do what is expected. _____
40. It is important to be generous and to do favors. _____
41. I like to talk about my achievements and experiences. _____
42. I have criticized others publicly. _____
43. I enjoy telling others how to do their jobs. _____
44. I enjoy accomplishing difficult tasks. _____

45. One should always be kind, sympathetic, and forgiving. ____
46. I often seek help and encouragement from others. ____
47. I don't mind dealing with all the details of my work. ____
48. I like having fuss made over me when I'm hurt. ____
49. I want to be noticed by others. ____
50. I often attack contrary points of view. ____
51. I enjoy settling arguments and disputes. ____
52. Above everything else, I want to be successful. ____
53. Others should always have an empathetic understanding of my problems. ____
54. I do everything to avoid interruptions. ____
55. It is important to conform to custom and avoid the unconventional. ____
56. Others readily confide in me about their problems. ____

Self-Esteem
Answer yes or no to each of the forty questions below.

1. I usually put my best foot forward. ____
2. I seldom feel embarrassed. ____
3. I feel I have above-average intelligence. ____
4. I am quite ambitious. ____
5. I can be very decisive. ____
6. I am tenacious in matters that count. ____
7. I enjoy my own company. ____
8. I have strong powers of concentration. ____
9. I don't feel shy or ill-at-ease with new people. ____
10. When outside situations beyond my control go wrong, I don't blame myself. ____
11. I enjoy receiving praise or compliments. ____
12. I don't get overly anxious when I have to address a group. ____
13. I feel I have good taste. ____
14. I have fantasies of doing something great. ____
15. I don't feel humiliated or get hurt if someone cracks a joke at my expense. ____
16. I don't mind showing off my good points and getting attention for them. ____
17. My general level of energy is high. ____
18. I can be quite assertive. ____

19. I enjoy taking calculated risks. ——
20. I have a lot of psychological toughness. ——
21. I have a great deal of self-confidence. ——
22. I can remain quite cool in a crisis. ——
23. I have considerable powers of discernment. ——
24. I am quite self-sufficient. ——
25. I feel I'm a persuasive person. ——
26. I like the way I look. ——
27. I feel I can hold my own in any group. ——
28. I can give compliments easily with sincerity. ——
29. I don't feel anxious when the boss calls me in. ——
30. I appreciate constructive criticism. ——
31. I am not easily hurt. ——
32. I am accepted by most people I meet. ——
33. I don't feel uncomfortable in a position of authority. ——
34. I choose my friends on the basis of their personality, rather than their credentials. ——
35. My friends value my friendship. ——
36. I am not overly preoccupied about my health. ——
37. I feel I have a strong personality. ——
38. My memory is good. ——
39. I react quickly and well to an unexpected situation. ——
40. If I'm good at something, I feel comfortable letting others know about it. ——

5 Building Your Skills Profile

You cannot be a fully functioning creative manager without knowing what best suits you. To find out, you must determine your actual skills, not the skills you wish you had or believe you have. The following three exercises will help you pinpoint what you do best and translate the findings into more effective management.

Skills are crucial to creative management because they constitute your problem-solving prowess. The greater and more varied your skills, the more problems that you can solve. The more problems you can solve, the more effective you can be and the further you can go in your career.

When identifying your skills, keep in mind that you need not use a skill continuously or exclusively for it to qualify as a bona fide skill. You may be very good at something you are called on to use infrequently.

Also, do not confuse knowledge with skill. For example, you might be able to explain what bicycle riding entails, but still not be able to ride a bicycle. On the other hand, you may not know the first thing about bicycle riding, yet do an excellent job of riding a bicycle the first time you try.

Do not overlook "invisible" skills. Many important skills are taken for granted simply because they are used so frequently or because they don't go beyond common sense. Yet, such skills can be critically important to accomplishing complicated tasks. Identifying them so that they can be used to increase your value may take a little practice, so be prepared to dig deep into your memory regarding what you do and have done.

Skills can be grouped into three basic categories. *Functional* skills are general capabilities that are useful for coping with the work environment. Examples include organizing, controlling, communicating, developing, planning, managing and motivating. *Adaptive* skills are personal capabilities that relate to self-management. These include creativity, discipline, dependability, persuasiveness, drive, memory, persistence, intuition, initiative, resourcefulness and perceptiveness. *Professional* skills are related to work content. They constitute know-how or the ability to use what you know. These areas of expertise include advertising, public relations, computer programming, financial management, accounting, marketing, sales, labor relations, law, etc.

Your most important skills are the ones that you have used effectively in the past. They can be identified by listing and analyzing ten of your most important achievements. These achievements should have involved considerable challenge. In making the list, be as specific as possible. For example, "managed the marketing department for three years" does not zero in on exactly what made the achievement significant. Strive for statements such as "increased department creativity/productivity by 30 percent" or "secured a new account worth $2 million."

From the list of ten major achievements, select the four most important ones. For each achievement, write down who else was involved, the factor or factors that motivated you to perform so well, and the precise roles that you played.

Then go to achievement tables I, II and III on the following pages. Tables I and II list functional and adaptive skills. The first four columns represent your four most important achievements. Put a check beside the skills you used in each of your four achievements, then add up the checks in each row and put the totals in the fifth column.

Table III will show the professional or technical skills that are specific to your work. Because these skills are unique to your job requirements, you have to write them in. Once you have listed your professional or technical skills in the space provided, complete the exercise as you did in tables I and II.

After completing these exercises, ask yourself which skills were used most often. Have you been aware that these skills play an important part in your career progress? Do these skills come easily to you? Where are your deficiencies? Can these deficiencies be remedied easily or is a change in your personality or behavior required?

You may have excellent skills that were not used much in your major achievements. (Or you may have serious deficiencies that have not shown up previously because you have not been required to use them or have avoided using them.) Thus, to get a more complete picture of your repertoire of skills, an analysis and profile of your skills is necessary.

Return to the three tables and focus on the six columns to the right of each skill. Consider each skill in light of your total work and personal experience. Rate yourself on each skill by marking a large dot in the appropriate box. (One is the lowest rating, five is the highest.) If you are unsure how you rate in a particular skill, place a check in the question mark box. After completing the rating process for each table, connect the appropriate dots for each skill. What you have drawn is a skills profile.

Last, but not least, you can utilize the insights you gained with your strengths and limitations to set a new career goal. In the last column in each table, rate the skills you need to achieve your goal according to the following scale:

1–2 Least important
3–4 Below average
5–6 Average
7–8 Above average
9–10 Extremely important

Table I
FUNCTIONAL SKILLS

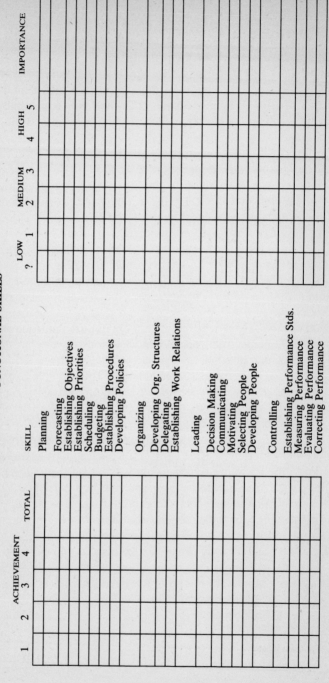

ACHIEVEMENT 1 2 3 4   TOTAL

SKILL

LOW ? 1   **MEDIUM** 2 3   **HIGH** 4 5   **IMPORTANCE**

Planning
Forecasting
Establishing Objectives
Establishing Priorities
Scheduling
Budgeting
Establishing Procedures
Developing Policies

Organizing
Developing Org. Structures
Delegating
Establishing Work Relations

Leading
Decision Making
Communicating
Motivating
Selecting People
Developing People

Controlling
Establishing Performance Stds.
Measuring Performance
Evaluating Performance
Correcting Performance

Table II
ADAPTIVE SKILLS

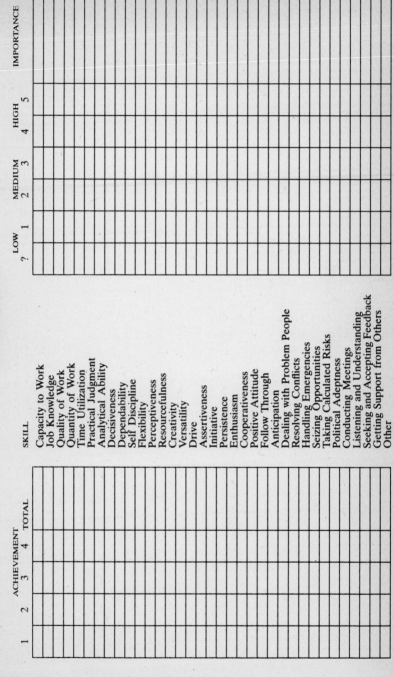

ACHIEVEMENT 1	2	3	4	TOTAL	SKILL	LOW ?	1	MEDIUM 2	3	HIGH 4	5	IMPORTANCE
					Capacity to Work							
					Job Knowledge							
					Quality of Work							
					Quantity of Work							
					Time Utilization							
					Practical Judgment							
					Analytical Ability							
					Decisiveness							
					Dependability							
					Self Discipline							
					Flexibility							
					Perceptiveness							
					Resourcefulness							
					Creativity							
					Versatility							
					Drive							
					Assertiveness							
					Initiative							
					Persistence							
					Enthusiasm							
					Cooperativeness							
					Positive Attitude							
					Follow Through							
					Anticipation							
					Dealing with Problem People							
					Resolving Conflicts							
					Handling Emergencies							
					Seizing Opportunities							
					Taking Calculated Risks							
					Political Adeptness							
					Conducting Meetings							
					Listening and Understanding							
					Seeking and Accepting Feedback							
					Getting Support from Others							
					Other							

Table III
TECHNICAL SKILLS

| ACHIEVEMENT | | | | | SKILL | | LOW | MEDIUM | | HIGH | | IMPORTANCE |
1	2	3	4	TOTAL		?	1	2	3	4	5	

6 | The Possible Dream

Even our best-laid plans, objectives, and dreams frequently change or get lost behind the haze and hurry of practical, or urgent concerns. Daily life with constant happenings tends to modify our situations—sometimes to the detriment of our well-being—and the only way we can retain leverage on our time, concerns and needs is to pry them loose for reassessment.

> ON SEPARATE SHEETS OF PAPER WRITE YOUR AN-SWERS TO THE FOLLOWING QUESTIONS CON-CERNING YOUR PAST, PRESENT, AND FUTURE.

PAST

1. What activities have provided you with the most enjoyment in your life?

2. How much time do you spend with these activities?

3. What were some of your past aspirations about which you felt extra good?

4. What has happened in your life that you wish never had happened?

5. What would you do differently if you could live your life over?

6. What basic themes run through the events in your life?

7. What were the most significant decisions in your life, and how did they turn out?

8. What was lacking in your life during those times when you felt especially bad?

9. What did you do to overcome these feelings?

10. What have you done really well and what did you learn from doing it?

PRESENT

1. What do you value most in your present life?
2. What kinds of events or activities give you the most satisfaction?
3. What do you do that makes you feel full of energy?
4. What do you believe is preventing you from doing what you really want to do?
5. What conflicts or problems do you have about the present? (Which ones did you personally create, and which ones were primarily caused by circumstances beyond your control?)
6. What specific changes should you make in order to move in the direction of a most satisfying life?

FUTURE

1. Do you have a fantasy or daydream that keeps recurring? (If so, does it relate to your life or job?)
2. What are some aspirations that you would like to fulfill? (If there are any constraints or limits in your present situation, what could you do to overcome them?)
3. What would you like to do really well?
4. What would you most like to accomplish before you die?
5. What career status do you visualize for yourself five years from now?

---

7 Visualizing Your Goals

One of the most common experiences in pursuing an important goal is that managers start out with a burst of enthusiasm and energy, and then quickly run out of steam. Visualization can prevent this. Through repeated visualization sessions, during which you practice and develop your goal images, you can continue to be highly motivated until you've reached your goal. But the value of visualizations goes even beyond sustaining motivation.

Many empirical reports by creative managers who practice visualizations regularly show that the ability to imagine and deeply feel what it would be like to achieve a goal will establish momentum and accelerate progress toward that goal. Internalizing the achieved goal images you create enables you to fully mobilize your inner resources and marshal previously untapped abilities. Visualization also liberates natural energies which are far beyond those you normally assume are available for you.

With repeated visualization you will be giving a highly positive program to your own biocomputer. This stimulates your subconscious to be continuously alert to situations that will further you toward your goal and to act assertively in those situations.

The following guidelines will help you to master this effective method of deepening and expanding your progress toward what you have chosen as your new goal.

SETTING THE STAGE

· Find a tranquil place where you will be totally undisturbed. Distracting external stimuli should be at a minimum.

· In addition to finding a quiet physical place, try to purge your mind, as far as possible, of ordinary concerns and preoccupations. Put aside matters that are not directly pertinent to your visualization and find a quiet mental space.

· Lie down with your legs uncrossed and your arms at your sides. Close your eyes and take a slow, deep breath, expanding your chest and lower abdomen. Pause for a moment. Then exhale slowly and feel your chest and abdomen relax. Breathe this way until you feel deepening relaxation. As you become progressively more relaxed, your breathing will become slower and more even, and you'll feel a comfortable calmness.

· Feel your feet and legs and imagine that they are becoming quite heavy. Say to yourself, "My feet and legs are becoming more and more relaxed. They are now deeply relaxed." Pause a moment and repeat this procedure with your ankles, thighs, pelvis, stomach, back, and chest. Rest a moment. Then relax your hands, forearms, upper arms, and shoulders. Pause a moment. Then relax the muscles of your neck and jaw. Allow your jaws to drop. Relax your tongue, cheeks, eyes, and forehead. Rest and enjoy the feeling of total relaxation.

· To go even deeper into a relaxed state, imagine yourself alone in an elevator. Watch the doors close and imagine looking at the panel which indicates the floor level. Imagine that number ten is lit up. Feel the descending motion as the elevator begins to go down. As the elevator passes each floor, you'll become more and more relaxed, going to a deeper, calmer level of your mind. With each number you visualize lighting up, you become calmer and more relaxed. When you "see" number one lighting up, you are at a deep, open state of mind.

· As you see the elevator doors open, you'll find yourself in a comfortable, dimly lit room. On the wall, facing a comfortable chair, is a large screen. Visualize yourself sitting in the chair facing the screen. Now you are ready to start your goal-visualization.

GOAL VISUALIZATION

· With eyes closed, create at least three distinct images in which your goal is already a present reality. Visualize the *full and complete result* you want. And make sure you visualize the terminal result and not a process of moving toward the result.

· Believe that the outcome you visualize is already achieved. A positive belief reinforces a positive outcome. Focus your will and your energy behind your visualization. Develop the images; get excited about them to the point where you actually believe their realness. It is vitally important that you believe in your images; they will be, as a result, more vivid and stable.

· Create images that are sharp, clear, intense, and filled with as many details as possible. Concentrate on the details. If your mind should wander, bring it slowly back to the images you created. Multifaceted visualization of your achieved goal will give multiple impressions to your subconscious, making your actual goal-attainment so much easier. Make sure, however, that your images are sharp and clear. Clear visualization will help you to clear away the mental fog which frequently obscures one's actual efforts and actions toward the goal.

· Let your entire being be aware of what is there. Experience the feelings you associate with having achieved your goal. Include visual, verbal, emotional, and mental aspects of the achieved goal.

Listen for sounds, touch, and smells. Be in the scene. Move around in the scene and picture all the details. Picture and describe yourself after you achieved your goal. What would you be doing? Feeling? Saying? Choose a *total* effect which includes the *circumstances* of having achieved the goal and the consequences of having it.

· Believe strongly that you absolutely *deserve* to achieve the goal you are imagining. Always visualize in positive terms and give yourself positive mental suggestions.

· Arrange to have your visualization sessions at least three times a week. Through repeated visualizations of a well-defined goal, your mind will begin automatically to set the course toward goal-attainment and to compensate when you get off course. With repeated visualizations you can also make any desired changes and perfect the result you seek.

Continue visualizing your goal as long as you wish. When you want to return to your everyday consciousness, simply go back to the elevator and return to the tenth floor, then open your eyes and you will feel rested, strong, and energetic.

---

8 | Fear of Failure

One category of managers who do not give themselves full permission to succeed are the failure-fearers. Many managers are held back from using their full potential because of their lack of faith in their ability to succeed. To be sure, some managers claim they have the needed self-confidence to succeed and that the prospect of failure doesn't bother them, but this is mere lip service. When asked why they haven't started to pursue an important project, they respond with all kinds of excuses or complaints about the obstacles and difficulties that stand in the way: too little time, pressing other obligations, lack of resources, corporate restrictions, and so on.

Managers with marked fear of failure tend either to set for

themselves modest goals or, in the other extreme, to pursue goals that are so difficult and way out that no one could blame them if they failed to reach them. Some managers hide their deep sense of inadequacy behind a highly self-aggrandizing image. They develop all kinds of grandiose and unrealistic plans, pursue them by fits and starts, and when it finally dawns on them that they're pursuing the impossible, their sense of failure and inadequacy breaks through their self-protective armor of grandiosity.

Even those managers who are not plagued by exaggerated self-doubts and thoughts of failure tend to be somewhat unrealistic in their estimation of themselves, and of the challenges they face. They usually overestimate the difficulties and underestimate their own abilities for resolving them. As a result, they make only half-hearted efforts when pursuing desired objectives. Underestimation of potential is largely responsible for the vacillation and excessive caution some managers show. Hesitation and caution are not, in themselves, bad, but if continued over a period of time, they have the propensity to strengthen negative projections of outcome, which can snowball into a self-fulfilling prophecy of failure.

Failures, mistakes, and setbacks are an integral part of achievement. It is doubtful that any manager ever really succeeded without taking risks. And risks inevitably entail some failure experiences. In the final analysis, what counts is not our mistakes and failures, but our emotional *willingness* to risk and accept failure. Strange as it may seem, when we have the courage to risk personal rejection, wasted effort, and even psychological defeat should our efforts fail, we've taken a giant step toward liberating ourselves of the fear of failure. And once we are free of this fear, there is almost an immediate upsurge of energies to exercise our capacities. Frequently we discover capacities we didn't even know we had, and that far exceed our expectations. Freed from the fear of failure, we're not only free to do our best, but to discover what its farthest reaches may entail.

To determine whether your career may be hampered by fear of failure, take the following test. Be honest with yourself. Do not guess how a successful creative manager might respond.

A Agree
B In-between or don't know
C Disagree

1. The surest way to get disappointed is to want something too much. ———
2. I seldom consult with my associates before deciding to go ahead with a project. ———
3. When I decide to go after something, I usually get it. ———
4. Before I decide what procedures to use in my work, I like to ask my peers for advice. ———
5. I sometimes downgrade my abilities so other managers won't expect too much from me. ———
6. When someone I know succeeds at something, I often feel I could have done as well, or better. ———
7. I don't mind having to ask other managers for things. ———
8. I seldom participate in competitive games. ———
9. When I have to complete an important project in a hurry, I get so upset that I can't concentrate on it. ———
10. I feel most of the time that I do things as well as I can. ———
11. I prefer to settle for less than I want rather than get into an argument about it. ———
12. I dislike people who look out for themselves first. ———
13. When I commit myself to something, I go through with it. ———
14. I can easily concentrate on a task for a long period of time. ———
15. Often, when I sit down to solve a problem, I get distracted and my thoughts drift off to other things. ———
16. My work tends to pile up so much that I have difficulty completing all of it. ———
17. I have little trouble saying no to people. ———
18. I like to explore subject areas in which I have little knowledge. ———
19. I have what it takes to be a success in management. ———
20. While developing a new idea I often tend to get stuck at a certain point. ———
21. I like to avoid situations where there could be potential conflict. ———
22. Even when I have good ideas, I frequently don't follow through on them. ———
23. I don't mind working on difficult problems, even when I'm not sure I can figure them out. ———
24. When I'm in a heated discussion, my mind often goes blank. ———

25. When starting to work on an important project, I
often find many other things that should be taken care
of first.   _____

To check your score, see the scoring instructions on page 135.

---

9 | Other Uses

The creative manager is fluent in his thinking and has the ability to
generate and juggle a large number of ideas when confronting a
problem or when seeking improvements. He can think of more
ideas in a given span of time than do managers who are less creative. Capable of tapping his imagination to scattershoot possibilities in volume, he stands a better chance of eventually
selecting and developing the significant ideas.

Here is a chance for you to exercise your fluency.

> LIST ALL POSSIBLE USES FOR A BUTTON OR BUT-
> TONS (ALL SHAPES AND SIZES).

---

10 | Verbal Dexterity I

Creative managers not only have rich vocabularies, but they also
display greater versatility with language. The following exercises
will loosen up your vocabulary and increase your associative
powers as well as your flexibility and resourcefulness of thinking
and expression.

Part One: THINK OF A WORD THAT FOLLOWS THOSE IN THE FIRST TWO COLUMNS AND PRECEDES THOSE IN THE LAST TWO. (YOU CAN FORM COMPOUNDS, HYPHENATED WORDS, COMMONLY USED EXPRESSIONS, COLLOQUIAL USAGE, OR SLANG IN SOME CASES.)

Example

Chicken	Rotten	Egg	Yolk	Head
Hold	Sit	_____	Squeeze	Rope
Act	Look	_____	Money	Set
On the	Daily	_____	Play	Jeopardy
Clock	Penny	_____	Up	Guy

Part Two: WHAT GEMSTONE IS CONCEALED IN EACH SENTENCE?

Example

Don't *rub y*our eyes with dirty fingers.

- You can't stop a Zen Buddhist from seeking enlightenment through introspection.
- Even if we walked a hundred miles, we still would have to stop a long way from our destination.
- The boss's habit of always calling Jane "my sugar" nettled Jane, although she never showed it.

Part Three: THINK OF A FIFTH WORD THAT IS RELATED TO THE PRECEDING FOUR WORDS. (YOU CAN FORM COMPOUNDS, HYPHENATED WORDS, OR COMMONLY USED EXPRESSIONS).

Example

Power	Series	War	Bank	World
Out	Up	Rich	Dumb	_____
Bean	Quartet	First	Along	_____
Let	Go	Cart	Broke	_____
Dock	Rot	High	Clean	_____
Circle	Rehearsal	Maker	Down	_____

Fight	Gone	Top	Ear	_____
Guard	Main	English	Builder	_____

> **Part Four:** ALL THE EXPRESSIONS BELOW HAVE SOMETHING IN COMMON. CAN YOU FIND IT?

China	Napalm
Ellipse	Allegory
Mistletoe	Ariboflavinosis
Diagnose	Keyed up
Alarm	Badmouth
Brown	Wheelbarrow

> **Part Five:** PUT TWO LETTERS IN THE BLANKS IN EACH SET TO MAKE THREE WORDS.

Example

_Ch_ air	Cat _ch_ y	Brun _ch_
_____ ce	B _____ go	Pard _____
_____ ror	H _____ e	Pe _____
_____ it	A _____ ect	Cla _____
_____ n	Ex _____ ct	A _____
_____ ter	P _____ try	Vass _____

> **Part Six:** GIVE A SYNONYM FOR EACH OF THE WORDS BELOW. THE SYNONYM HAS TO BEGIN WITH THE LETTER H.

Example

Custom	Habit
Accord	_____
Cheerful	_____
Occur	_____
Crop	_____
Own	_____
Danger	_____
Assist	_____
Elevated	_____
Conceal	_____

11 Peripatetic Women

Most effective problem solvers habitually generate many different possible explanations for situations they observe around them. Only after they have amassed a great number of possibilities do they narrow them down to a few most likely explanations to test their validity.

Poor problem solvers, on the other hand, tend to make snap judgments as to problem causes. They rest content with only one or two plausible explanations and then turn to other matters.

Here is a statement which is presented as a fact, although it may or may not be true. Nevertheless, give as many plausible explanations as you can to account for the phenomenon.

> RESEARCH HAS REVEALED THAT WOMEN CHANGE JOBS ALMOST TWICE AS OFTEN AS DO MEN. WHAT ARE THE POSSIBLE REASONS FOR THIS?

12 Suggestion Systems

Various suggestion systems to stimulate ideas from employees have had a long history, but the results have been mostly disappointing. At the inception of a suggestion system there is usually a flow of ideas to help a company, but then the flow trickles to a halt.

Try to come up with at least ten to fifteen specific steps.
Include ways in which in-house publications could be utilized.

13 Like/Unlike

Original communication requires the knowledge of a rich array of
synonyms and antonyms. This exercise will increase your ability to
be more creative and successful in their use.

FOR EACH WORD GIVE A SYNONYM BEGINNING
WITH THE LETTER "R."

Example:
   Actual   real
   1. discard   _____
   2. sane   _____
   3. look   _____
   4. sparkling   _____
   5. plausible   _____

   Now give synonyms beginning with the letter "C."

   6. profession   _____
   7. quote   _____
   8. disaster   _____
   9. outcome   _____
   10. calculate   _____

Now give synonyms beginning with the letter "H."

11. agreement   _____
12. customary   _____
13. dupe   _____
14. innocuous   _____
15. bargain   _____

FOR EACH WORD BELOW WRITE ONE THAT MEANS THE OPPOSITE. EACH ANTONYM MUST BEGIN WITH THE LETTER "D."

---

1. crawl   _____
2. fragile   _____
3. vacillate   _____
4. conceal   _____
5. uniformity   _____

Now give antonyms beginning with the letter "M."

6. reduce   _____
7. small   _____
8. generous   _____
9. inconspicuous   _____
10. succeed   _____

Now give antonyms beginning with the letter "P."

11. defective   _____
12. discontinue   _____
13. turbulent   _____
14. tasteless   _____
15. uncertain   _____

14 What Could It Be?

This exercise will help you in developing associational fluency.

> USING THE COLUMNS BELOW, SELECT ONE WORD
> FROM THE FIRST COLUMN AND ONE WORD FROM
> THE SECOND COLUMN. THEN IDENTIFY AS MANY
> THINGS AS POSSIBLE THAT POSSESS THESE TWO AT-
> TRIBUTES. FOR EXAMPLE, SOMETHING HOT AND
> MOBILE MIGHT BE A HAIR DRYER, A JET ENGINE,
> OR THE SUN.

Try to use at least ten different two-word combinations. Once you have mastered these, try it with one word from the first column and two words from the second.

hot	mobile
cold	silvery
large	wooden
small	metallic
fast	electrical
slow	glass
square	slippery
round	rough
expensive	transparent
inexpensive	flexible

15 Odd One Out

Most problems belong to classes of problems. If we make an error in classification we fail to solve the problem. The process of classification helps us to retrieve information in an accurate manner for creative problem solving.

WHICH WORD IN EACH SET DOES NOT BELONG TO THE SAME CLASS WITH THE REST?

---

1. inch   yard   meter   mile   foot
2. temper   discourtesy   impoliteness   rudeness   impudence
3. slacks   pants   shorts   trousers   Levi's
4. turquoise   navy   lavender   indigo   sapphire
5. France   Korea   Japan   China   Siberia
6. nicotine   anesthetic   drug   sedative   opiate
7. answer   response   reply   acknowledgment   contradiction
8. Giants   Cardinals   Dodgers   Indians   Pirates
9. basketball   tennis   baseball   football   lacrosse
10. courage   politeness   gentility   refinement   courtesy
11. fluorescent   incandescent   candle   moon   gas
12. four   nine   sixteen   twenty-five   thirty
13. subtract   reduce   diet   dilute   weaken
14. oak   elm   maple   mahogany   pine
15. attack   stroke   assault   sally   raid
16. highway   avenue   street   boulevard   parkway
17. football   soccer   hockey   baseball   basketball
18. polyester   Acrilan   nylon   wool   rayon
19. jade   coral   amethyst   quartz   turquoise
20. Paris   London   Rome   Athens   Monte Carlo

16 Are You Intuitive?

You have a tough decision to make, a real problem to come to grips with. Where do you start? Usually with the facts of the situation. You pore over the details, scrutinizing, hashing, rehashing. You want to do what's right and take no detail for granted. You put your trust in logic and objectivity. Every move is orderly, calculated, step-by-step.

Suddenly, you get a strong gut feeling. A hot flash of intuition blazes across your mind. You regard it as an impulse and realize that it has nothing to do with the facts or details of the situation, but for some reason it *feels* like a promising solution. So what do you do? Go with it, logic be damned? Or shrug it off and keep squinting at pros, cons, and other cumbersome details?

If that flash in your mind seems too simple, if you say to yourself that hunches are no match for cool objectivity, you may be discounting your most dependable problem-solving tool. Recent research reveals that although intuitive thinking is one of the most useful modes of creative problem solving, it is too often neglected and brushed aside. Whether employed in the world of work or in everyday life, sharp hunches can pay off in a big way.

The following self-test provides you with a measure of your present level of intuitive ability. Mark your answers as accurately as possible. Try not to second-guess how an intuitive manager might respond to each statement.

TRUE FALSE

1. I think that, other things being equal, a logical, step-by-step method is still the best way for solving problems. ___ ___
2. Good hunches have provided the impetus for many of my successful projects. ___ ___
3. I have lived to regret many of my actions and decisions that went counter to my intuitive feelings. ___ ___
4. In order for me to act upon a decision, it has to "feel right." ___ ___

70

5. In my experience, intuitive hunches have proven
to be unreliable guides for action.   ___ ___

6. I feel that many of my ideas seem to grow out of
their own roots, as if independent of my will.   ___ ___

7. I have very little interest in problems that do not
have clear-cut answers.   ___ ___

8. I regard myself as unconventional, independent,
and spontaneous, and I enjoy taking risks.   ___ ___

9. I have the ability to penetrate to the essence of a
situation.   ___ ___

10. When I get a hunch, I feel compelled to act on it. ___ ___

11. I tend to rely on the feeling of "rightness" or
"wrongness" when moving toward the solution of
a problem.   ___ ___

12. Many of the penetrating insights I have experienced have been touched off by seemingly insignificant coincidences.   ___ ___

See scoring and analysis on page 143.

---

17 Taking Charge of Your Time

We cannot stop the flow of time, or reverse it, or slow it down.
Everyone has been given just 24 hours a day. Some creative managers are able to achieve extraordinary things during this period;
others don't have time to think. The secret is effective time management and the management of choices of what are attended to.
Performance-conscious managers know how to get the most of
their time and energy and how to allocate it effectively. They've
been able to get rid of the energy leaks and fluff that reduce the
effectiveness of so many of their colleagues.

71

The circle below represents your typical workday. It is divided into four quarters, each quarter representing two hours. Estimate how many hours or parts of an hour you spend on your projects and tasks.

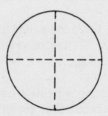

This exercise provides you with a first inventory of how you spend your time. You might ask yourself the following questions:

- What changes would I like to make in the various sizes of the sections to salvage more time?
- What could I actually do to change the size of the various activity sections?

Next you need to make a careful analysis of your *actual* daily performance and activities. Since most managers' reconstructed estimates of how they use their time are not entirely accurate, you should begin by auditing and analyzing the way you spend your time on a daily basis—over a period of one or two weeks. Separate routine activities from intermittent tasks, and creative and productive activities from nonproductive ones. This meticulous analysis will concretely demonstrate where and how you spend your time productively, and how you misallocate and mismanage it. It will give you a basis for making effective changes. You will be able to identify the high and low payoffs of your efforts and establish a more appropriate priority system.

You can use the following time analysis chart, or construct one of your own.

Time	How time was spent	Degree of necessity for achieving an important objective Scale of 1–10 not necessary to essential	Degree of usefulness in achieving an important objective Scale of 1–10 not necessary to essential

Utilize the insights derived from past use of time to prepare a plan that allows your time to be spent more effectively. This plan should, first of all, include your new daily work schedules. It should incorporate your work objectives, and the short-term activities and steps you need to reach them. It should list both your regular and objectives-related tasks in order of their priority and the time allocated for each task.

Part Two   LIST AT LEAST 20 TO 30 SPECIFIC THINGS
YOU COULD DO TO CONSTRUCT A MORE EFFECTIVE
TIME-MANAGEMENT PROGRAM FOR YOURSELF.

Examples:

• Have my secretary screen all my phone calls.
• Cut down on phone time.
• Start meetings on time even if someone is missing.

73

- When reading a letter, jot down points of reply.
- Sharpen time estimates for tasks I have to accomplish.
- Set up in-basket system according to priorities.

Now it's your turn.

18 Are You Under the Right Amount of Stress?

Of all the feelings that seriously hamper creative problem solving, excessive stress ranks first.

Most creative managers are flexible and tough, and can stand considerable amounts of stress and strain. Yet, it is estimated that over one third of the managers in the corporate world experience, at one time or another, stress that impairs their creativity to a degree where they can no longer function efficiently.

Most managers regularly face urgent situations in their work and, as a matter of course, get keyed up to meet the problems. Soon after the "crisis," however, they are able to relax. Some managers can relax within two or three minutes after the stress-producing situation ends. Others may take a few hours. But they are *able* to relax.

The trouble comes when the manager can't relax, when his overmobilized body refuses to return to normal, when blood pressure stays high and muscles stay cramped. Even though the "threat" is no longer present, the manager is on edge, all wound up.

HEALTHY STRESS

Most of us have experienced normal excitement, the kind that happens when we've solved a difficult problem, or when we have to attend an important meeting to decide on a course of action. The stress we experience on such occasions is healthy. We need it

74

to be motivated, to be alert, and we also need it to put forth constructive effort in pursuit of our objectives. Thus, not all stress is harmful.

Actually, a certain amount of stress, which varies from individual to individual, can even be healthy. It can keep us alert and exhilarated, galvanizing us to action. There are creative managers who actually thrive on stress and who consider it "the spice of life."

On the other hand, stress that *persists* on a high level is definitely harmful. In a vital sense, stress can be likened to strong medicines: the right dose can save a life; excess amounts are like poison.

STRESS THRESHOLDS

Thresholds for stress vary. A stress-producing situation for one manager may be a motivator or stimulator to another. One individual can take a great deal of pressure and show no ill effects, while the same pressure would be incapacitating to another. The difference lies in how a manager reads the situation. There are managers in seemingly impossible environments who nevertheless cope superlatively well.

We all have our own optimum stress-tolerance level. If we go beyond it, we become irritable, impatient, and inefficient. If we go far beyond it, we become disorganized and, in the end, incapacitated. If we are below our optimum stress level, we fail to fulfill our creative potential, and if we are far below it, we just "string along," or we vegetate.

In general, we shouldn't worry about stresses that are transient. The real erosion of our emotional and physical well-being happens when stresses come in clusters, when they pile up, or when a worrisome circumstance is unduly prolonged. These overloading situations strain our capacity to cope and we may succumb to serious states of unwellness.

THE SYMPTOMS OF STRESS

A variety of symptoms accompany stress. In its high form we tend to be irritable, ill at ease, constantly tired; we do not enjoy life and tend to magnify even slight frustrations into major disasters. We also tend to become forgetful, are unable to concentrate, and are prone to lack of objectivity in our perception of situations.

We may feel that we are working hard, but this becomes mere wheel-spinning, and we accomplish little. We show excessive concern over unimportant details and are unable to delegate work. We procrastinate. Finally, we get into argumentative moods toward our associates.

In addition, we may engage in obsessive ruminations about our own work performance and may end up with a feeling of "what's the use." Various aches and pains, particularly backaches, also accompany persistent stress.

STRESS QUIZ

The following quiz will enable you to determine how vulnerable you are to stress, how much stress there is in your life right now, and how well the stress is handled.

Respond to each question honestly, checking off the answer that most accurately describes the situation as it actually is, not as you would like it to appear, or think it should be. Frank answers will give you the most reliable feedback on what, if any, readjustments in attitudes, feelings, and behavior are required to restore emotional well-being, or what stressful situations should, if possible, be avoided.

	OFTEN	SOME-TIMES	SELDOM	NEVER
1. During the past three months, how often were you under considerable strain or pressure?	—	—	—	—
2. How often do you experience any of the following symptoms: palpitation or racing heart, dizziness, painfully cold hands or feet, shallow or fast breathing, restless body or legs, insomnia, chronic fatigue?	—	—	—	—
3. Do you have headaches or digestive upsets?	—	—	—	—

	OFTEN	SOME-TIMES	SELDOM	NEVER
4. How often do you experience pain in your neck, back, arms, or shoulders?	—	—	—	—
5. How often do you feel depressed?	—	—	—	—
6. Do you tend to worry excessively?	—	—	—	—
7. Do you ever feel anxious or apprehensive even though you don't know what has caused it?	—	—	—	—
8. Do you tend to be edgy or impatient with your peers or subordinates?	—	—	—	—
9. Do you ever feel overwhelmed with feelings of hopelessness?	—	—	—	—
10. Do you dwell on things you did, but shouldn't have?	—	—	—	—
11. Do you dwell on things you should have done, but didn't?	—	—	—	—
12. Do you have any problems concentrating on your work?	—	—	—	—
13. When you're criticized, do you tend to brood about it?	—	—	—	—
14. Do you tend to worry about what your colleagues think of you?	—	—	—	—
15. How often do you feel bored?	—	—	—	—
16. Do you find that you're unable to keep your objectivity under stress?	—	—	—	—

	YES	NO
17. Of late, do you find yourself more irritable and argumentative than usual?	—	—
18. Are you as respected by your peers as you want to be?	—	—
19. Are you doing as well in your career as you'd like?	—	—
20. Do you feel you can live up to what top management expects from you?	—	—

77

21. Do you feel your spouse understands your problems and is supportive of you? ___ ___

22. Do you have trouble with any of your associates? ___ ___

23. Do you sometimes worry that your associates might be turning against you? ___ ___

24. Is your salary sufficient to cover your needs? ___ ___

25. Have you noticed lately that you tend to either eat, drink, or smoke more than you really should? ___ ___

26. Do you tend to make strong demands on yourself? ___ ___

27. Do you feel that the limits placed on you by top management regarding what you may or may not do, are just right? ___ ___

28. Are you able to take problems in stride, knowing that you can deal with most situations? ___ ___

29. Do you seldom "lose your cool" and stay productive under stress? ___ ___

30. Do you feel left out in meetings? ___ ___

31. Do you habitually tend to fall behind with your work? ___ ___

32. During the last year have you, or anyone in your family, suffered a severe illness or injury? ___ ___

33. Have you recently moved to a new home or community? ___ ___

34. During the last three months, have any of your pet ideas been rejected? ___ ___

35. Is it very difficult for you to say no to requests? ___ ___

36. Do you generally work better when under pressure? ___ ___

37. Are you able to focus your concentration when under pressure? ___ ___

38. Are you able to return to your normal state of mind reasonably soon after a stressful situation? ___ ___

For scoring instructions and analysis, turn to page 150.

19 | Match Point

Many problems needing creative solutions require that the parts of the problem be rearranged into a new pattern. These exercises increase your ability to make transformations in visual terms. To work them successfully, you have to move one or more matches to a different position to make the equations correct, or to get the required configurations. For example, if matches are laid out in this pattern,

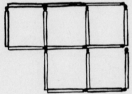

remove three matches and leave three squares. The solution is:

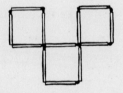

1. Move one match and make this equation valid.

2. Remove two matches and make this equation valid.

3. Move one match and make this equation valid.

$$||| - || = |V$$

4. Move one match and make the equation valid. There are two solutions.

$$V| - |V = |X$$

5. Eighteen matches form a Solomon's seal which comprises eight triangles. Move two matches and reduce the number of triangles to six.

6. Move one match and make this equation valid.

$$V - |V = V||$$

7. From this row of six matches, shift two so as to leave nothing.

8. Move one match and make the equation valid.

$$X - | = |$$

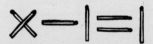

80

20 Coping with Neophobia

To enable you to bring about effective organizational change, you must gain insight into the dynamics of resistance. Determining the causes will help you to adopt appropriate measures to overcome resistance.

The most common resistance to new ideas stems from people's opposition to change. Even routine changes in organizations create resistance. It is easy to imagine how much a radically new idea creates. Whoever said "Creation is a stone thrown uphill against the downward rush of habit" did not exaggerate.

Any organization that wishes to survive has to have rules, regulations, and controls to channel the actions and behavior of its individual members into an orderly routine. Without planned routine the organization would lapse into chaos. Thus, a certain amount of *inflexibility* is necessary to accomplish organizational objectives.

Creative ideas and innovation, however, upset organizational order and are, therefore, often regarded with inhospitable and intolerant attitudes. Yet, without innovation organizations could not stay viable for long.

> WHAT ARE THE MAIN REASONS FOR THE RE-
> SISTANCE TO NEW IDEAS AND CHANGE? WHAT ARE
> THE CONDITIONS THAT MUST BE MET TO INTRO-
> DUCE CHANGES?

21 Smugnosis

Elbert Hubbard once observed that "the world is moving so fast these days that the man who says it can't be done is generally interrupted by someone doing it." And he is dead right. Historically there is ample evidence to prove that the affliction of *smugnosis* has been widespread. For example, in 1945 the famous scientist Vannevar Bush told the President a couple of months before the first successful testing of the atomic bomb: "The bomb will never go off, and I speak as an expert in explosives." Lee DeForest, who was instrumental in developing TV, predicted: "While technically TV is feasible, it will never be a serious competitor to radio. The average American family just doesn't have time for it." Edwin Land, the inventor of Polaroid camera, was advised by experts to kill it because it would be too expensive as a toy and not up to snuff as a camera.

While not perhaps as dramatic, many ideas are killed in American business daily by all kinds of idea-squelching judgments. These negative comments effectively serve to block new ideas, staunch the flow of future suggestions, and prevent the acceptance of even carefully prepared new ideas.

LIST ALL THE IDEA SQUELCHERS YOU HAVE HEARD OR PERSONALLY EXPERIENCED, OR EVEN YOURSELF USED ON OCCASION.

Examples:

- It's been done this way for ten years—why change?
- I know it won't work.
- That's been tried before.

22 Decisions, Decisions

One of the key functions of the managerial process is decision making. Almost all managerial tasks—planning, organizing, controlling, executing, delegating, motivating and developing subordinates—involve problem solving and arriving at decisions.

While there are many variations in the styles of decision making, two distinctly different types of decision makers—perhaps at opposite poles—stand out. While both types may have good knowledge of the decision-making process and possess the requisite skills, one differs from the other basically in having an attitude of confidence with which he or she makes decisions.

Although considerable risks may be involved, the more effective manager has confidence that his decisions can and will translate into effective action. He has the courage to make estimates of probability and take calculated risks even when a sufficient number of facts are not available. The basic attribute of the effective decision maker is the ability to select among many alternatives the best course of action, even though none of them is a sure bet.

The indecisive manager, on the other hand, frequently experiences inordinate anxiety when weighing alternatives. He knows that a decision cannot be reached automatically by simply adding up the facts—there are never enough. Yet, he does not trust his intuitive hunch, which plays a major role in most decisions. It should be remembered that in decision making there are no certainties, only probabilities.

Some managers have such a fear of making a wrong decision that they feel it is better to make no decision at all. These managers should be advised that no executive always makes good decisions. It is the batting average and the willingness to modify a bad decision, rather than cover it up, that counts.

Many managers sell short their decision-making ability by uncritically accepting the many faulty notions about the decision-making process.

LIST AS MANY MISCONCEPTIONS ABOUT DECISION MAKING AS YOU CAN. LIST THOSE YOU MAY HAVE WITNESSED IN OTHERS AS WELL AS THOSE THAT MIGHT HAVE HAMPERED YOUR OWN DECISION MAKING.

23 Who's in Charge Here?

The classic story of the Caine Mutiny illustrates one of the important lessons of management: an aggressive team of subordinates can turn on their comparatively weaker leader and bring him down to failure and humiliation. The essential ingredient to the mutiny, as the story unfolds, is that the leader is passive and vacillating and the aggressive crew tries to step in and fill the power vacuum.

However, the story of the Caine Mutiny only illustrates one of the many possible manager-subordinate power patterns. Every individual manager, as well as his or her key subordinate, can be characterized as occupying a position on a continuum of power-related behavior that ranges from *passive,* at one end of the scale, through *assertive* in the middle, to *aggressive* at the opposite end of the scale. The place where a boss and each of his subordinates match up on the continuum provides a useful index for predicting how a boss-subordinate pair will behave toward one another—whether they will have a successful working relationship or one that is marked by conflict and dissension. The astute creative manager is well advised to have a full understanding of how power and dominance issues affect his work. Knowing how he matches up to the power behavior of his subordinates can frequently make the difference between success and failure.

Although no one is purely passive, purely assertive, or purely aggressive, for the sake of convenience it is useful to select these three points on the scale to describe the boss-subordinate interactions and typical behavior as it relates to power, dominance, and the maintenance of the pecking order.

Passiveness is displayed by someone who is typically withdrawn, tries to be a nice guy, wants to be liked, doesn't like to compete, and feels inhibited when responding to power challenges. Charlie Brown of cartoon fame is a good example of this wishy-washy personality.

Assertiveness can be defined as standing up for oneself, getting what one wants most of the time without either running roughshod over others or waiting for permission to pursue one's

84

rightful objectives. It is a competitive attitude. Assertive people like to win and they know that the main ingredient in organizational environments, whether it involves implementing a change or gaining acceptance of a new idea, is power.

Aggressiveness can be defined as the chronic use and abuse of others for one's own ends, with little or no concern for the harm inflicted on others' lives and careers. It is a no-holds-barred, fiercely competitive, win/lose battle, and it is often less a case of competition than destructiveness, and not so much of winning as wanting to make others lose.

There are nine essential or dominant patterns of boss-subordinate interactions:

1. The passive boss and the passive subordinate.
2. The passive boss and the assertive subordinate.
3. The passive boss and the aggressive subordinate.
4. The assertive boss and the passive subordinate.
5. The assertive boss and the assertive subordinate.
6. The assertive boss and the aggressive subordinate.
7. The aggressive boss and the passive subordinate.
8. The aggressive boss and the assertive subordinate.
9. The aggressive boss and the aggressive subordinate.

Expressed in a matrix or grid, the pattern of interaction can be displayed this way:

		The boss's power behavior is typically expressed as:		
		Passive	Assertive	Aggressive
The subordinate's behavior power is expressed as:	Passive	1	4	7
	Assertive	2	5	8
	Aggressive	3	6	9

> WRITE OUT IN DETAIL HOW YOU THINK EACH OF THE NINE PAIRS INTERACT WITH EACH OTHER, AS WELL AS WITH OTHERS, IN A TYPICAL BUSINESS ORGANIZATION.

24 Test Your Work Pattern

To have work to do that is stimulating, exciting, and satisfying is one of the most fundamental sources of joy in this world. It is one of the few activities that consistently brings solid contentment.

Because many creative managers become so involved with their work, often to a point where many other aspects of their lives are relegated to the back seat, they have been accused of being workaholics. There is, however, considerable difference between workaholism and a dedicated pursuit of a career. Workaholic managers, even when blessed with considerable talent and skill, are locked into a state of constant anxiety. They are consumed by self-doubts about their talents and they tend to torture themselves with harsh and even merciless criticism. They are not inspired by a genuine desire to achieve, but are compulsively driven by a constant need to prove their worth to themselves and to others. This urgent need for reassurance makes them, in addition, extremely sensitive to what other people think of them, and they are constantly preoccupied with making a favorable impression. In contrast, truly successful managers enjoy their work, irrespective of what others may think of it. They also know that achievement requires an infinite capacity for taking pains.

There are managers who do not particularly like their work, but nevertheless work obsessively and almost without a pause. Many of them even admit that a vacation or unexpected idle time could drive them crazy. To be sure, almost every manager is occasionally faced with heavy workloads, short-term emergencies, and tight deadlines that are stressful. But the work-addicted managers tend to put off a breather for themselves not because of the demands of the job, but because of their own demands on themselves. These are the harried managers who talk fast, walk fast, and act as if slowing down to relax would be tantamount to failure.

This can have harmful consequences. It can preclude living a well-rounded, balanced life with many interests outside the world of work. It can ruin personal relationships and result in an added psychological stress of isolation. And it can put a manager's career itself in a self-destruct mode. Work overload leads to gradual wearing down of reserves, with little recharging of energies. This can lead to mental, physical, and emotional exhaustion, known as burnout.

The following test is designed to determine your work behavior patterns. Respond to each question honestly, checking off the answer that most accurately describes your behavior and feelings as they actually are, not as you would like them to be or think they should be. Frank answers will give you the most reliable feedback and make the test results more useful for you.

1. Do you take work home and work late into the night?
   a. ___often   b. ___ sometimes   c. ___ never
2. Do you work on weekends and holidays?
   a. ___often   b. ___ sometimes   c. ___ never
3. Do you get to work early to get a jump on things?
   a. ___often   b. ___ sometimes   c. ___ never
4. On Monday mornings are you
   a. ___ anxious to get back to work?
   b. ___ reluctant to start another week of work?
   c. ___ Neither anxious nor reluctant?
5. Would you say that
   a. ___ there are too many inappropriate demands on your time?
   b. ___ the demands on your time are not excessive?
   c. ___ you could undertake many more projects?
6. Do you have to skip or shorten your lunch breaks?
   a. ___often   b. ___ sometimes   c. ___ never
7. Do you ever work while you eat lunch?
   a. ___often   b. ___ sometimes   c. ___ never
8. Do you find that you are harassed by constant, unexpected emergencies?
   a. ___ yes   b. ___ no
9. Do you move, walk, and eat rapidly because you don't want to waste even a minute?
   a. ___often   b. ___ sometimes   c. ___ never
10. Would you say that you feel
   a. ___ pretty much in control of work problems most of the time?
   b. ___ sometimes in control?
   c. ___ harassed and not in control most of the time?

11. Do you find that you can't miss a day of work because you would fall too far behind?
    a. ___ yes   b. ___ no
12. Do you find it difficult to say no to requests?
    a. ___ often   b. ___ sometimes   c. ___ never
13. Is it important for you to do things better than other managers?
    a. ___ yes   b. ___ no
14. Do you feel you always have to be "on" at work?
    a. ___ yes   b. ___ no
15. Do you find yourself fretting when your subordinates do not "move at your command" or work as fast as you do?
    a. ___ often   b. ___ sometimes   c. ___ never
16. How would you rate yourself?
    a. ___ exceedingly ambitious
    b. ___ moderately ambitious
    c. ___ not ambitious at all
17. Do you strive for perfection and excellence?
    a. ___ often   b. ___ sometimes   c. ___ never
18. Do you have the freedom you need to perform your work the way you believe is best?
    a. ___ yes   b. ___ no
19. Are you able to set priorities with a proper sense of urgency and importance?
    a. ___ usually   b. ___ sometimes
    c. ___ never
20. If you were suddenly laid off, what would you miss the most?
    a. ___ the money
    b. ___ the work itself
    c. ___ the company of your colleagues
21. Would you say that your present work
    a. ___ underutilizes your abilities and skills?
    b. ___ overtaxes your abilities and skills?
    c. ___ allows you to grow and develop new skills?
22. At the end of a working day, do you feel
    a. ___ exhausted and fit for nothing?
    b. ___ glad that you can spend time on your personal life?
    c. ___ occasionally tired, but usually quite satisfied?
23. Do you find it difficult to relax and do nothing?
    a. ___ yes   b. ___ no

24. Do you feel vaguely guilty whenever you relax, especially when you're facing a deadline?

    a. ____often   b. ____ sometimes   c. ____ never

25. Do you find it difficult to enjoy leisure because you can't stop thinking about problems at work?

    a. ____often   b. ____ sometimes   c. ____ never

26. Do you find that leisure time bores you and that you'd much rather be at the office?

    a. ____ yes   b. ____ no

27. Do you find that you don't particularly like taking vacations?

    a. ____ yes   b. ____ no

28. Are you able to maintain a good balance between your work and your private life?

    a. ____ yes   b. ____ no

29. Do you talk about your work

    a. ____ on your free time with friends or family?

    b. ____ only with colleagues or the boss?

    c. ____ never

30. If you suddenly won a large sum of money, would you

    a. ____ quit working for the rest of your life?

    b. ____ pursue a different career?

    c. ____ continue in the same line of work as you do now?

To check your score and what it means, turn to page 169.

25 | Do You Fear Success?

There are managers who have a basic ambivalence about succeeding: they *want* but also want *not* to succeed. They suffer from fear of success.

While managers who have a marked fear of failure prefer to retreat from competitive situations, and from the risks involved in trying to improve their careers, success-fearing managers welcome success-oriented activities. Many of them are exceedingly ambitious and desire to be recognized for their achievements. But as soon as they've made any significant progress toward a desired objective, they feel a compulsion to check themselves and to find ways to sabotage success.

To determine whether your career may be hampered by fear of success, take the following test. Be honest with yourself.

A——Agree
B——In-between or don't know
C——Disagree

1. When things seem to be going really well for me, I get uneasy because I know it won't last. ____

2. Most of the time I find that I measure up to the standards I've set for myself. ____

3. I find it difficult to tell my friends that I excel at something. ____

4. It is important for me to be liked by people in positions of higher status and power than mine. ____

5. When I win a competitive game, I feel a little sorry for the other player. ____

6. When I have to ask others for help, I feel I'm imposing on them. ____

7. Although I may experience occasional difficulty doing so, I generally finish essential projects. ____

8. When I think I've been too forceful in making a point to a fellow manager, I get worried that I might have made him feel unfriendly toward me. ____

9. When other managers compliment me on my work, I feel they are being insincere. ____

10. When I complete an important piece of work, I am usually satisfied with the result. ____

11. When engaged in competitive games, I make more mistakes near the end than at the beginning. ____

12. When the chief executive officer praises my work I wonder whether I can live up to his expectations in the future. ____

13. At times I believe I have gotten as far in my career because of good luck, not because I deserve it. ____

14. It is just as important to win a game as to merely enjoy it. ____

15. I often daydream about accomplishing something that no one else has ever accomplished before. _____
16. I like being the center of attention in a social gathering. _____
17. Most of my fellow managers are secretly pleased when I get into trouble. _____
18. I'm pretty skillful at most things I try. _____
19. When I make a decision, I usually stick with it. _____
20. I often get excited when I start working on a new project, but it gets stale rather quickly. _____
21. I often feel let down after completing an important project. _____
22. At times my accomplishments amaze me because I feel that I rarely put in the effort that I could. _____
23. When I hear about the accomplishments of other managers, I tend to think how little I myself have accomplished. _____
24. I'm not influenced one way or another by persuasive people. _____
25. When a project seems to be going well, I often get scared that I'll do something to botch it. _____

To check your score, see the scoring instructions on page 171.

---

26 | Letters Will Do

Here's another chance for you to test your verbal facility in a creative way.

> PLACE THE APPROPRIATE NUMBER OF LETTERS IN THE BLANK SPACE TO DESCRIBE WHAT EACH STATEMENT INDICATES.

Example:
What two letters are a number?   __AT__ (eighty)

1. What two letters describe a snake's eyes? _____
2. What two letters mean rot? _____
3. What two letters mean not difficult? _____
4. What two letters mean all right? _____
5. What two letters mean cold? _____
6. What two letters mean a vine? _____
7. What two letters are a girl's name? _____
8. What two letters mean vacant? _____
9. What two letters mean jealousy? _____
10. What two letters mean an attractive girl? _____
11. What two letters are a written composition? _____
12. What two letters are a county in England? _____
13. What two letters are a tent used by American Indians? _____
14. What two letters mean to surpass others? _____
15. What two letters mean superfluity? _____
16. What letter means a great deal of water? _____
17. What three letters mean a funeral poem? _____
18. What three letters mean happiness? _____
19. What two letters mean a passage between sections of seats? _____
20. What two letters mean expensive? _____
21. What two letters mean compassion? _____
22. What three letters describe a person who flees from confinement? _____

27 What Does It Mean?

Knowing word meanings leads to the mastery of concepts. And concepts are important for thinking and creative communication.

1. erudite — cognizant profound literary scholarly
2. dogmatic — bigoted certain opinionated confident
3. nondescript — abnormal unnatural odd undefinable
4. gratuitous — unbiased exempt free independent
5. quandary — doubt crisis emergency dilemma
6. litigant — lawyer contestant libelant suitor
7. vacillate — oscillate vibrate undulate waver
8. jargon — slang cant tongue gibberish
9. debase — adulterate weaken humble depress
10. gullible — childish simple credulous trustful
11. validate — regulate honor test confirm
12. circumvent — baffle entrap deceive elude
13. crass — dense raw dull coarse
14. strident — grating hoarse guttural coarse
15. infringe — transgress purloin invade intrude
16. peremptory — binding conclusive tyrannical imperative
17. sobriety — steadiness abstention calmness temperance
18. servile — oily enslaved pliant obsequious
19. deprecate — protest belittle disapprove remonstrate
20. ululation — crying howling twittering yapping
21. upbraid — revile condemn reproach reject
22. quirk — dodge peculiarity evasion subterfuge
23. dauntless — spirited gallant intrepid fearful
24. robust — hardy solid unyielding tough
25. equanimity — serenity toleration poise patience
26. posthaste — rashly swiftly nimbly actively
27. gourmet — epicure trencherman gorger glutton
28. intuition — reasoning perception impulse apprehension
29. remiss — negligent indolent slow shiftless
30. motif — theme reason purpose inducement
31. hackneyed — trite habitual usual frequent
32. zealous — ready willing partisan ardent

93

28 | Who Owns the Zebra?

Creative managers are often faced with a plethora of seemingly unrelated facts and information. Yet they are able to manipulate and harvest the information, so that a valid solution emerges. The following exercise tests your ability to analyze and fit the information together for a proper solution.

1. There are five houses, each of a different color and inhabited by men of different nationalities, with different pets, drinks and cigarettes.
2. The Englishman lives in the red house.
3. The Spaniard owns the dog.
4. Coffee is drunk in the green house.
5. The Ukrainian drinks tea.
6. The green house is immediately to the right (your right) of the ivory house.
7. The Old Gold smoker owns snails.
8. Kools are smoked in the yellow house.
9. Milk is drunk in the middle house.
10. The Norwegian lives in the first house on the left.
11. The man who smokes Chesterfields lives in the house next to the man with the fox.
12. Kools are smoked in the house next to the house where the horse is kept.
13. The Lucky Strike smoker drinks orange juice.
14. The Japanese smokes Parliaments.
15. The Norwegian lives next to the blue house.

Now, who drinks water? And who owns the zebra?

29 | Nitty-Gritty

The ability to separate the relevant from the irrelevant can be an important skill in problem solving. Making such distinctions, however, can be very difficult, especially when we are dealing with familiar things. Nevertheless, we must learn to see things in terms of their usefulness to us. Otherwise we would be overwhelmed by the amount of information we would have to process.

> IF YOU WERE TO MAKE IMPROVEMENTS ON THE PRODUCTS THAT FOLLOW, WHICH ATTRIBUTES WOULD YOU CONSIDER TO BE RELEVANT AND WHICH WOULD YOU CONSIDER TO BE LESS RELEVANT?

1. Roller skates
2. Telephone
3. Calculator
4. Stapler
5. Light bulb
6. Typewriter
7. Bicycle
8. Doorknob
9. Toaster
10. Clock

30 Stretching Perspectives

The act of distorting a problem situation is another way to provide new problem perspectives and to develop unique solutions. Comedians rely heavily on distortion and exaggeration, since stretching the facts about a situation in an unusual or unexpected manner is the basis for many types of humor. The same principle can also be applied to more concrete problem situations. By simply listing the desired objectives for a problem and then exaggerating each one, a new way of looking at the problem is created that often will lead to a creative solution. It is not the type of exaggeration that is important, but rather, the fact that any exaggeration or stretching of the problem is attempted.

To illustrate, a problem of how to develop a better briefcase might be set up as follows:

Original Objective	Exaggerated Objective	Possible Solution
Lightweight.	No weight.	Use no metal; use self-reinforcing, vinyl materials.
Easy to open.	Always open.	Opens on touch; use outside pockets.
Secure from unauthorized entry.	Opens only for owner.	Voice-actuated locks.

Now here's a problem you can practice with:

DEVELOP A BETTER COPYING MACHINE.

31 | Linear Perspectives

One of the most useful of creative thinking modes is visual thinking. It is particularly useful in solving problems in which shapes, forms, patterns, and spatial relationships are concerned. Yet, it is often underdeveloped. This exercise will flex and liberate your visual imagination.

> UTILIZING ONLY SEVENTEEN STRAIGHT LINES, DRAW SOMETHING RECOGNIZABLE.

In addition to some more or less conventional pictures, try to depict some whimsical, intriguing, and clever patterns.

Examples:

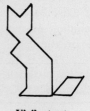

Vigilant cat

Punk hairdo

Sitting bullfrog

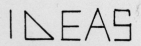

What we need more of

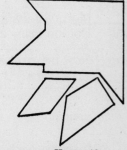

Honest Abe

32 | S(i)MILE
When You Say That

Creative managers almost naturally gravitate to the usage of metaphors, similes, and analogies in their thinking. As a result, their perceptions of situations are not only more colorful and evocative, but also more original.

Metaphor or simile has been considered, since antiquity, as one of the most potent tools for the creative worker. Aristotle stated that "the greatest thing by far is to be the master of metaphor." He regarded metaphoric ability, which implies perception or discernment of linkages and qualitative similarities between disparate phenomena and objects, as a mark of genius.

In technology, science, business, and problem solving in general, it is frequently a metaphor or simile that provides the key to a new invention or a new theory. Poetry, literature, and art, of course, could not exist without metaphors, because only the metaphoric mode is able to communicate the deeper reality and relationships, the "qualitative kinships" that exist between things. Thus, any radically new perception or meaning, no matter what the field is, tends to adopt a metaphoric expression.

> LIST AS MANY ANSWERS AS YOU CAN TO THE QUESTION: HOW IS AN ICEBERG LIKE A BIG IDEA?

Examples:

- Most of it doesn't show.
- Not too many around.

> NOW DO THE SAME WITH: HOW IS A METAL SPRING LIKE HOPE?

Examples:

- It springs back when it is down.
- It is resistant and flexible.

33 | Clustering Ideas

When a large number of possible problem solutions has been generated, it can be difficult to select only one or two to implement. This is especially true when there are several equally attractive alternatives. The time or other resources needed to implement more than one or two possible solutions isn't always available.

One way out of this dilemma is to combine and modify several ideas to produce just one or two final solutions. This is done by clustering similar ideas into categories and then compromising on two or more ideas within the categories to produce one workable idea. You then can work with successively more narrow categories until only three or four remain. Thus, you might initially start with ten or more categories and then gradually reduce these in number by combining some of them into broader categories.

Suppose, for example, that you generated the following uses for a one-gallon plastic milk container:

1. A funnel.
2. A flowerpot.
3. Storage for emergency water supply.
4. Disposing of used engine oil.
5. Party hat.
6. Bird feeder.
7. A flotation buoy.
8. Packaging material.
9. Toys for children.
10. Small-parts storage.

These ten uses could be categorized in three ways (among other possibilities): as a container (2, 3, 4, 6, 10); as a functional device other than a container (1, 7, 8); and as a decorative item (5, 9). These three categories then might be reduced to just two: containers and functional devices; decorative items.

The number of items could be further reduced by combining them within categories. Thus, a funnel and small-parts storage might suggest a funnel-type device for holding screws—whenever you need a screw you tap the device and a screw falls out.

TO TRY YOUR HAND AT THIS PROCESS, COMBINE
AND MODIFY THE FOLLOWING SOLUTIONS FOR A
PROBLEM ON HOW TO OBTAIN FUNDS FOR A NON-
PROFIT PRESCHOOL CENTER:

1. Have a telethon.
2. Have an auction.
3. Start a magazine.
4. Get company sponsors.
5. Solicit contributions from community fat cats.
6. Have a fund-raising carnival.
7. Baby-sit for a professional fund-raising organization in exchange for their services.
8. Have children collect donations door-to-door.
9. Have a concert.
10. Seek a federal grant.
11. Write a book.
12. Have a bake sale.
13. Take care of pets for a fee.
14. Make and sell ice cream.
15. Get a university film department to produce a fund-raising film to show on TV and to various community groups.
16. Solicit funds from rich relatives.
17. Make and sell toys.
18. Get free public-service announcements on TV and radio.
19. Publish a newsletter.
20. Have a raffle.

34 What If?

One of the most effective techniques for reawakening and liberating imagination is the "what would happen if . . ." game. It develops resourcefulness and helps one to break out of stereotyped and habitual thinking patterns.

WHAT WOULD HAPPEN IF ALL OF A SUDDEN THE SUN WOULD SHINE ONLY ON THE EARTH'S SOUTHERN HEMISPHERE, AND NOT AT ALL ON THE NORTHERN HEMISPHERE? WHAT ARE SOME OF THE THINGS THE FOLLOWING COMPANIES AND PEOPLE COULD DO TO STAY IN BUSINESS?

1. A manufacturer of suntan lotion?
2. A tour arranger for a travel agency?
3. An electric lamp manufacturing company in the southern hemisphere?
4. A zoo curator in the northern hemisphere?

35 | Verbal Dexterity II

The following games will give you another opportunity to increase your ability to perceive relevant relationships and to exercise your fluency and flexibility in the use of words.

Part One: THINK OF A WORD THAT FOLLOWS THOSE IN THE FIRST TWO COLUMNS AND PRECEDES THOSE IN THE LAST TWO. (YOU CAN FORM COMPOUNDS, HYPHENATED WORDS, COMMONLY USED EXPRESSIONS, COLLOQUIAL USAGE, OR SLANG IN SOME CASES.)

Steeple	Apple	_____	Pot	Knife
Big	Rotten	_____	Jack	Pie
Square	New	_____	With	Out
Beater	Plant	_____	Good	Easter

Part Two: WHAT GEMSTONE IS CONCEALED IN EACH SENTENCE?

If you have lots of time to tour, Mali, Nepal, and Bali can be included in the itinerary.

Jack said, "I am on drugs because of a medical condition."

Thou shouldst rename thy street after thy father.

Part Three: THINK OF A FIFTH WORD THAT IS RELATED TO THE PRECEDING FOUR WORDS. (YOU CAN FORM COMPOUNDS, HYPHENATED WORDS, OR COMMONLY USED EXPRESSIONS).

Time	Ribs	Minister	Number	_____
Angle	Wing	Hand	Triangle	_____
Time	School	Light	Break	_____
All	Fall	Cap	Club	_____
Land	Strings	Failure	Ache	_____
Cat	Head	Chance	Chew	_____

Part Four: PUT TWO LETTERS IN THE BLANKS IN EACH SET TO MAKE THREE WORDS.

____ art	C____tion	Cl ____
____ al	Vi____r	Con____
____ ter	Ex____ct	Aga____
____ ten	Al____t	Go ____
____ orous	Sh____e	Mad____
____ oll	C____chy	Wh ____

Part Five: GIVE A SYNONYM BEGINNING WITH THE LETTER H FOR EACH OF THE WORDS BELOW.

Obstruct _____

Frank _____

Sacred _____

Annoy   ——————
Chase   ——————
Affectation ——————
Supposition ——————
Available   ——————
Random   ——————
Valiant   ——————

---

36 | Sticky Fingers

Here's a hypothetical problem for you to use in applying your learnings from the previous exercises:

> ASSUME THAT YOU ARE THE PRESIDENT OF A LARGE CHAIN OF DEPARTMENT STORES. IN RECENT YEARS, SEVERAL OF THE STORES HAVE BEEN PLAGUED BY INCREASING LOSSES DUE TO SHOPLIFTING. IN WHAT WAYS MIGHT YOU REDUCE SHOPLIFTING IN THESE STORES?

Allow yourself plenty of time to work on this problem, devoting at least twenty minutes each day to it. After you have worked through the entire process, compare your responses with the partially worked-out example in Part II. You might find that some of the sample responses will suggest new ways of approaching the problem or new solutions. If you are stimulated by the example, go ahead and make any changes you wish to your own responses. Be careful, however, that you don't use the example as the correct approach or as your primary standard of comparison. The responses in the example are only representative of the types of responses that might be used. They definitely are not exhaustive, nor do they represent the only way the problem can be approached.

You can use the following questions as guides for helping you work through the problem. If you can think of any other considerations, go ahead and use them in your approach.

GETTING READY

1. How do you personally feel about this problem?
2. What do you know about shoplifting?
3. Can you develop mental images of someone shoplifting?
4. What would stores be like if there were no shoplifting?
5. What information do you need to solve this problem?
6. How might you go about collecting this information?
7. What are the major, essential characteristics of the problem?
8. Which characteristics of the problem are related?
9. Which characteristics of the problem are more important than others?
10. Who shoplifts?
11. What do shoplifters steal?
12. Where do people shoplift?
13. When do people shoplift?
14. Why do people shoplift?

WHAT'S HAPPENING?

1. Can you tune in to the problem to describe in sufficient detail what you would see, hear, touch, taste, or smell in shoplifting situations?
2. Can you vicariously experience the thoughts and feelings of a shoplifter at the moment of taking something?
3. What's good about shoplifting? In what ways might shoplifting benefit stores and/or other people?
4. Can you imagine the awareness levels of shoplifters, store employees, and customers in the store while a shoplifting act is occurring? How much do they see and hear at this time?
5. What different types of noises, lights, voices, etc. might attract or deter shoplifters?
6. How would you define the problem at this point?

LOOSENING UP YOUR MIND

1. What are the constraints of this problem?
2. What assumptions do most people make about shoplifters and shoplifting?
3. Can you challenge any of these assumptions? How?
4. What cultural taboos might help shoplifters?
5. What elements of shoplifting are similar to one another? What elements are different?
6. What else is like shoplifting?
7. What reversals can you think of to describe the shoplifting problem?
8. How can you exaggerate the objectives of a shoplifting reduction program?
9. What fantasy solutions to the problem can you develop?
10. What is the silliest possible solution? What practical solution can you develop from this?
11. Look over all your responses. In what ways might you redefine the problem now?

LETTING GO

1. How many different solutions can you think of in ten minutes?
2. For the moment, forget about the shoplifting problem. In five minutes, how many different ways can you think of to prevent people from doing something? Do any of these ideas suggest possible solutions to the shoplifting problem?
3. Select five different objects from your immediate environment. Giving yourself three minutes for each object, how many different solutions can you think of that might be suggested by the objects?
4. Look over your list of solutions. Can you combine any to produce new solutions?

BEING DIFFERENT

1. What makes you angry about shoplifting? In what ways might you change these factors to develop problem solutions?

2. What new names can you think of to describe your solutions to this point? Do these names suggest new solutions?
3. Can you use the different characteristics of a light bulb to suggest possible solutions?
4. Write a brief, one-or two-paragraph story about shoplifting. Make it silly, if you wish. What new ideas are suggested by this exercise?
5. What is different about your solutions?
6. Can you think of any improvements that could be made on previously tried solutions?

YOU'RE THE JUDGE

1. What values are relevant to shoplifting incidents?
2. Can you reduce the total number of solutions you have generated to three to five categories? Can you combine any of these solutions?
3. What criteria will your solutions have to satisfy in order to solve the problem?
4. How important are each of these criteria relative to the others?

---

37 How Well Do You Listen?

Most of us accept the premise that good listening is crucial to effective communication. Yet, studies show that only about 10 percent of us listen properly; most of us don't know how to, or don't want to, listen intelligently, systematically, and purposefully. Even good listeners are not always operating at peak listening efficiency.

It was shown in an experiment that took place in a school system, with participation from first grade through twelfth grade, that good listening deteriorates with age.

During the experiment the teachers were asked to interrupt

themselves suddenly at certain times and to ask their students two questions: "What was I talking about?" and "What were you thinking about?" Over 90 percent of first and second graders were shown to be listening and hearing what the teachers were saying. In junior high school, only about 44 percent were listening and hearing what the teachers were saying. In high school, from tenth through twelfth grades, the percentage dropped to only 28 percent!

Most people talk at one another rather than with one another. Each person thinks he is making meaningful points, but rarely do they add up to genuine communication.

There are at least six reasons for being a good listener:

- We learn a great deal by listening.
- It helps us solve problems creatively.
- It gives us time to think.
- It increases our self-confidence.
- It helps us sell ideas.
- It generates new ideas.

Listening generates lots of ideas. Indeed, by far the most effective method by which managers can tap other people's as well as their own ideas is by attentive listening. Nothing can equal a genuine willingness to listen.

THE LISTENER IS IN THE DRIVER'S SEAT

It is generally assumed that the speaker is more important than the listener in carrying on meaningful communication. Certainly both are vital. Yet, analysis of the communication process reveals that the listener is, indeed, the more important link.

To most people, listening consists of trying to figure out as fast as possible the central point of the other person's message. The trouble is that this central point is frequently screened and distorted by the listener's preconceptions. He tunes out as soon as he thinks he has grasped the gist of the message, then mentally prepares his own statement on the topic he assumes is being discussed.

Each listener interprets and visualizes what he hears, and then reacts and responds to his interpretation. If his interpretation is at

107

odds with the speaker's meaning, good communication stops or, at best, slows down considerably.

Many laboratory experiments have demonstrated shortcomings in listening. A typical test, involving six subjects, proceeds as follows: Five subjects leave a room. The remaining one is exposed to a picture of a street scene and is given two minutes to study and memorize as many details as he can. The picture is then withdrawn. The second subject is then called into the room, and the first subject describes the picture to him. He in turn tells the third subject what he heard, and this goes on until the last subject is reached.

The last subject describes the picture as he visualizes it, based on the description he has heard. When he is actually shown the picture, he does not recognize it. Why?

This is what usually happens to the message transmission: 1. Fewer details are passed on each time the picture is described. 2. Details are distorted or changed. 3. One subject's inferences are transformed into definite assertions as he or she passes on the description to the next person. 4. Each subject emphasizes different details in his or her description.

EVALUATE YOUR LISTENING HABITS

Here's a quiz to identify your own irritating listening habits in order to pull the plug on them. It will enable you to measure your own or someone else's listening ability. Gutsy managers can have their subordinates and superiors evaluate their listening habits. This, of course, not only takes great self-confidence, but also some self-assurance that one is a good listener and communicator.

COMPLAINTS	OFTEN	SELDOM	NEVER
1. Doesn't give me a chance to explain fully what my problem is.	___	___	___
2. Never lets me complete more than a few sentences before interrupting. Acts as if it is hard to wait for me to finish.	___	___	___
3. Likes to finish sentences for me.	___	___	___
4. Being questioned about what I've just said indicates I wasn't listened to at all.	___	___	___

5. Often gives me the feeling I'm
   wasting time by talking.   ⎯⎯ ⎯⎯ ⎯⎯

6. Never smiles while I'm talking, so I
   feel uncomfortable.   ⎯⎯ ⎯⎯ ⎯⎯

7. Seldom looks at me while I talk, so it
   is hard to tell whether I'm being
   listened to.   ⎯⎯ ⎯⎯ ⎯⎯

8. Sneaks looks at the clock or watch
   while I'm talking. Often acts as if
   something else is more important
   than what I have to say.   ⎯⎯ ⎯⎯ ⎯⎯

9. Constantly cleans fingernails or
   fiddles with an object, gazing at it
   rather than listening to me.   ⎯⎯ ⎯⎯ ⎯⎯

10. Has a knack for steering me off my
    subject with questions and
    comments.   ⎯⎯ ⎯⎯ ⎯⎯

11. Whenever I make a suggestion or
    propose an idea, the immediate
    reaction is "No."   ⎯⎯ ⎯⎯ ⎯⎯

12. Always tries to anticipate what I'm
    going to say, jumping ahead of me to
    tell me what I had in mind.   ⎯⎯ ⎯⎯ ⎯⎯

13. Rephrases what I say in such a way
    that my meaning is completely
    distorted.   ⎯⎯ ⎯⎯ ⎯⎯

14. Stares at me whenever I talk, as if
    disbelieving everything I have to say.   ⎯⎯ ⎯⎯ ⎯⎯

15. Has a way of putting me on the
    defensive or confusing my thinking
    whenever I ask a question.   ⎯⎯ ⎯⎯ ⎯⎯

16. Almost everything I say triggers an
    argument, even before I've had a
    chance to explain fully what I had in
    mind.   ⎯⎯ ⎯⎯ ⎯⎯

17. Tries to be flip when I have
    something serious to discuss.   ⎯⎯ ⎯⎯ ⎯⎯

18. Looks at me in an evaluative or
    critical way when I speak, making me
    wonder whether something is wrong
    with me.   ⎯⎯ ⎯⎯ ⎯⎯

19. Never stops doing the task at hand to
    turn attention to me completely when
    I approach with a question.   ___ ___ ___

To check your score and what it means, turn to page 194.

---

38 Overcoming Managerial Isolation

As the manager rises in the corporate hierarchy, he is increasingly prone to become isolated from his subordinates. The result is a blockage in the flow of information he needs to function effectively.

The first step in eliminating managerial isolation is to specifically define the areas you want to be informed about. You cannot allow yourself to be occupied only with those matters that others decide to bring to your attention. You must take the initiative.

> **Part One:** LIST ALL THE STEPS YOU COULD TAKE TO IMPROVE COMMUNICATION BETWEEN YOU AND YOUR SUBORDINATES.

> **Part Two:** WHAT SPECIFIC DIRECTIVES COULD YOU ISSUE TO YOUR SUBORDINATES TO REDUCE ISOLATION? WRITE DOWN AT LEAST FIVE SPECIFIC DIRECTIVES.

39 | Strictly for the Birds

This series of C.B. (Creativity Barrier) Birds, drawn half in fun and all in earnest, represent some of the strange vertebrates whose counterparts are still found in many businesses. A fully developed and dominant C.B. Bird can easily wreck a creative team, a department, or even a company. He (or she) does it by crippling a free exchange of ideas, by hindering the development of new ideas, or by stifling any innovative expression.

> WRITE YOUR OWN BRIEF DESCRIPTIONS OF THE BIRDS DEPICTED BELOW. EACH ONE SHOULD REPRESENT IN ITS OWN INDIVIDUAL WAY HOW NEW IDEAS GET BLOCKED.

Examples:

This bird likes to perch on subordinates' shoulders to make sure that the tasks he assigns are completed *his* way. In his opinion, his ideas are the only ones of any importance. Being directive and autocratic, he likes to pull rank whenever he can, and with his threats, orders, and demands he scares subordinates into complete submission.

This bird is a relentless hair-splitter. His preferred mode is to counter and dispute the meaning of every utterance with "I don't agree," or "Well, no. . . ." He likes to interrupt, nitpick, and point out only the flaws in other people's ideas. He is generally grumpy, humorless, and sees only the gloomy side of everything. Often he ends up flying alone in ever decreasing circles and meets himself . . . in the end.

After attempting your own versions of the two birds above, give your descriptions of the following five birds.

40 | Problem Situations

The creative manager has keen powers of observation and an unusual ability to perceive and notice deficiencies, difficulties and challenges that have escaped the attention of others. He also has greater sensitivity toward the unusual or the promising aspects of situations—the hidden opportunities often not perceived by others. The exceptional, incongruous, or paradoxical situations that occur snap him instantly to attention and are grist for his mill.

Because the creative manager is more sensitive to problems, he tends to be dissatisfied with things as they are and eager to improve upon them. Hence he is constantly either seeking or finding challenging problems to solve. For him there is hardly a situation entirely free of problems, but this does not cause him frustration or worry. On the contrary, he welcomes the challenge of problems and the state of happy dissatisfaction with the status quo.

> ON A SEPARATE PIECE OF PAPER, LIST ALL THE PROBLEM SITUATIONS IN YOUR ORGANIZATION. ASK IN WHAT WAYS WE CAN . . .

Examples:
Streamline and accelerate the work flow.
Assure consistent customer satisfaction.

41 | Blocks and Barriers

Deficiencies in creative problem solving do not necessarily indicate the absence of creative potential. In most cases they are the result of the many blocks and barriers that tend to inhibit, distort, and discourage effective creative thinking.

Luckily, once the barriers have been identified, and a conscious effort is made to remove them, the immediate upsurge of creative output can be considerable.

In a sense, the problem can be likened to a gutter under the eaves of a roof, clogged with dead leaves, twigs, bugs, and sediment. In order for the rainwater to flow through, the gutter must first be cleared. In a similar way, free-flowing creativity and receptivity to new ideas also require the elimination of cognitive, perceptual, emotional, and environmental barriers.

Although gaining insight into most blocks is sufficient to make more productive use of one's latent creative talents, there are some personal blocks that are not only difficult to recognize in oneself, but are difficult to admit and to overcome, even in one's own best interests. However, facing them in a conscious, open way, and regarding them as problems and challenges to solve, moves one toward a more creative life-style.

LIST ALL THE BLOCKS (ENVIRONMENTAL, COGNITIVE, PERCEPTUAL, EMOTIONAL) THAT IMPEDE CREATIVE THINKING AND PROBLEM SOLVING.

---

42 | Managing Creative People

While there is little doubt that top management sets the overall tone of the creative climate in most business and industrial organizations, the one key person who directly influences the welfare of the creative personnel is their immediate manager. This is the person who is in daily contact with a staff of creative people and who, by constant interaction and the relationship established with them, provides the daily atmosphere where creativity emerges and grows, or withers and dies. It is the creative manager's stimulating guidance and inspiring leadership that constitute the most potent motivational influence on creative output.

> DESCRIBE WHAT SPECIFIC ATTITUDES AND ACTIONS ARE NECESSARY FOR THE EFFECTIVE MANAGEMENT OF CREATIVE PERSONNEL.

43 | Teamwork Dynamics

Almost everyone agrees that teamwork makes for a more productive and potentially more creative work situation, but few managers can put their fingers on why.

> **Part One:** IN YOUR OPINION, WHAT ARE SOME OF THE MOST IMPORTANT BENEFITS AND CHANGES THAT TEAMWORK CAN BRING ABOUT IN AN ORGANIZATION, AND WHY?

The job of creating a well-integrated team is never done. The creative manager must constantly be on the lookout for ways that will make his team more productive and efficient.

> **PART TWO:** LIST SOME OF THE FACTORS THAT CONTRIBUTE TO TEAM EFFECTIVENESS AND PRODUCTIVITY. HOW WOULD YOU CHANGE THE ATTITUDES AND BEHAVIOR OF RECALCITRANT TEAM MEMBERS?

44 Closed/Open Systems

Many of the functions that an effective manager of creative personnel performs depart radically from the standard philosophy and principles of management. For example, decision making involving the creative staff has to be participative and representational, rather than centralized or unilateral. For another thing, the manager's role is less that of an agent or representative of top management and more that of a communicator and representative for the creative staff.

While management has been traditionally viewed as production-centered, with creative staffs it must be employee-centered. According to the old philosophy, the task to be performed and the production goals to be met are the pivotal factors, and the responsibility falls upon the manager for seeing to it that the job is done to specifications. In the new, emerging pattern of managing creative staffs, the responsibility for getting the job done or the problem solved is shifted to the individual creative employee, and the manager's task is transferred from policing to helping, from issuing orders and commanding to coaching and motivating.

The new emerging open-system style of managing creative personnel entails greater recognition of and responsiveness to the intrinsic motivations and characteristics of individuals. With the open system, there is also less control over the direction of activities, and fuller utilization of creative individuals in the decision-making and problem-solving processes. It has become increasingly evident that without active encouragement for initiative in problem solving and maximal participation in refining organizational purposes and goals, the creative staff fails to achieve the necessary clarity and autonomy which alone can permit truly creative performance. Cognizant of this, the creative manager, together with top management, works at establishing open-system conditions which give a greater latitude for initiative and responsibility to creative people, and which relax the external controls of their performance. Thus the creative manager has the responsibility for creating a climate that will make each creative employee more self-directing and responsible, and more capable of utilizing his or her talents and skills to the full.

The following instrument enables you to measure whether the existing organizational system in your company facilitates or inhibits creativity.

> USING A SCALE OF 1 (MOST CLOSED) TO 10 (MOST OPEN), RATE YOUR PRESENT ORGANIZATIONAL CLIMATE VARIABLES IN THE FOLLOWING AREAS.

The Closed System

A. High hindering, albeit unobtrusive; reluctant sharing to downright withholding of resources and information; veiled obstruction and mild sabotage. Defensiveness and exaggerated concern for personal security, power, and status. Self-centeredness and an inability to admit one's weaknesses or mistakes.

The Open System

A. High helping; needs of all employees are addressed; high sharing of resources and information. Freedom from defensiveness and preoccupation with power, status, or security. Self-abandoning task orientation and freedom to admit one's mistakes.

117

The Closed System	The Open System
B. Moderate to high rejection of influence, suggestions, and requests. Avoidance of openness or revealing of differences.	B. High acceptance of influence and suggestions; high responsiveness to requests. Free interplay of differences without personal conflict. —
C. Moderate to low communication: primarily task-oriented; guarded and defensive; often destructive, critical, ridiculing.	C. High communication: open, honest, effective, persuasive, spontaneous, undefensive, constructive, and empathetic. —
D. Conflicting goals and interests over an extensive domain; emphasis on power and outcome differences; and, often, commitment to each other's defeat. Mutual, reciprocal fear and distrust.	D. Common goals, shared interests and commitment to each other's goal-attainment; focus on the striving member. Growth producing relationships. —
E. Ambiguous and variable motives and intentions; frequently untrustworthy, hostile, resentful, and destructive, resulting in frustration, disappointment, bewilderment, and withdrawal.	E. Trustworthy, friendly and helpful motives and intentions. Warm feelings toward others; appreciation, satisfaction, cooperation, and involvement. —
F. Status and ability differences emphasized and exaggerated; similarities minimized if not virtually denied.	F. Mutual similarities emphasized and shared; realistic assessment of others' strengths and weaknesses; acceptance of differential expertise; complementarity of different role skills valued. —

The Closed System	The Open System
G. Conformity and lack of spontaneity, initiative, innovation, experimentation, or curiosity.	G. Spontaneity, initiative, creativity, originality, innovation, experimentation, and curiosity.
H. Emphasis is on winning; solidarity is disvalued; specific task activities; failure, defeat, and distress of the other frequently desired.	H. Solidarity; good feelings, interests of other engineers taken into account; wide range of task-related activities; group tasks and products.
I. Self-concept has very few dimensions; self-esteem unstable, defensive, and strongly affected by perception of rival and by winning and losing. Results in caution, inflexibility, and inability to relinquish the old and explore the new.	I. Self-concept has many dimensions; high, stable self-esteem, which frees the person to be flexible, to entertain new ideas, to be objective and creative.
J. Strong desire to win; excitement of competing; desire to increase status and cause others the pain of one's own success. Use of power over others; dictatorial and arbitrary decisions. Negativism, pessimism, cynicism.	J. Completion of tasks and subtasks; desire to maintain solidarity, help others, and not let down members; enjoyment of interaction and "we-feeling"; competence motivation. Shared power, participative decision making and problem solving. Positivism, optimism.

45 How to Evaluate Ideas

Many ideas fail in the marketplace because they are flawed. Frequently, a detailed and systematic evaluation would have corrected the defects. Yet, it is amazing how many managers still evaluate new ideas in a haphazard fashion.

People produce lots of ideas in organizations. The problem frequently is not a dearth of ideas, but the ability of managers to distinguish between just ordinary ideas and good ones. It is only through thorough evaluation that we can separate the good from the bad and the promising from the merely probable. Proper evaluation can prevent the unprofitable pursuit of ideas that are inherently unworkable. It can save money, energy, and time.

This exercise is designed to provide you with a screening tool you can use to evaluate the worth of new ideas—either those you come up with, or the ones your associates or subordinates propose to you.

> FORMULATE A DETAILED CHECKLIST OF QUESTIONS
> THAT WOULD ENCOMPASS ALL THE CRITERIA YOU
> WOULD WANT TO USE TO EVALUATE IDEAS.

Examples:

- How timely is the idea?
- Is it feasible in terms of cost?
- Can people afford it?
- How desirable is the market for this new product or service?
- Will the demand for the product or service grow?

46 The Politics of Selling Ideas

An idea must be sold to those who have the power to decide what to do with it. Rarely can ideas, plans, and proposals be sold without the support of several key managers or top executives.

A fact of life that many managers seem to deny is that people in organizations are hierarchical and political by nature, rather than fair and equalitarian. Even a fairly simple dialogue between a key executive and a manager is a hierarchical one and appropriate manipulative skills are needed to get your idea past the barriers of self-interest that your superior may erect.

The hard, prickly fact is that ideas frequently upset the political/power structure of an organization. One would think that "an idea is simply an idea." This is wrong, for an idea can also be a dithering device that threatens the apportionment of power among those with hierarchical positions in the organization.

The following test measures how well you can handle the rough and tumble of selling and pushing your idea to get the attention of top decision makers.

A——Mostly true
B——Mostly false

1. Power in organizations is one of the most important factors for achieving acceptance of ideas. _____
2. One's professional skills and knowledge enhance idea-selling efforts. _____
3. Being power conscious or politically astute is destructive and denotes a desire to manipulate others. _____
4. On balance, good ideas are more important to success than are power and politics. _____
5. It is impossible to figure out what will motivate a person to support my idea. _____
6. Colleagues should be prepared to help one another to gain the acceptance of an idea. _____
7. A good idea is often defeated by irrelevant issues. _____

8. When there is a difference of opinion about the value of an idea, a logical argument is usually sufficient to settle the difference. _____

9. I should not have to polish the apple to get a hearing for my ideas. _____

10. Getting one's idea accepted is a matter of luck. _____

11. To protect a good idea of mine, I'm willing to argue with my boss. _____

12. I'd rather have the support of senior decision makers than the favor of my coworkers. _____

13. Even when one disagrees with a top executive, it is better not to show it publicly. _____

14. When presenting an idea, it is important to act and look composed even when one is not. _____

15. A fair idea-review system would insure that my contribution to the organization would be recognized. _____

16. A boss's power must always be taken into consideration when planning a presentation of an idea. _____

17. People who stoop to playing power and politics to promote their ideas are usually untalented or incompetent. _____

18. Rather than generate resistance, it is always better to clear an idea with those affected before acting. _____

19. When I propose an idea, I am unlikely to encounter resistance, except on the most important issues involved. _____

20. The higher the level of my personal contacts in the organization, the better the chances are for my ideas to succeed. _____

21. When I propose a good idea, it is inevitable that people will naturally fall into pro, neutral, and con attitudes about it. _____

22. The best way to sell an idea is to package it so that it fits the biases of the audience, even if it compromises the idea a bit. _____

23. The appraisal of one's idea has nothing to do with power and politics. _____

24. If I don't get the cooperation I need to get my idea accepted, it is probably because I don't use the proper tactics and strategies of persuasion. _____

25. When presenting an idea, it is better to look friendly rather than hostile, even to those I oppose or do not like. ____
26. When selling an idea, any time is about as good as any other. ____
27. I usually go to my company's social events to make points, even when I'd rather be doing something else. ____
28. It is usually a waste of time to try to speak up in meetings and expect to have any influence. ____
29. The higher the level of the decision maker I can reach, the better are the chances for my idea to survive. ____
30. At idea presentations, it is at times appropriate to raise questions about the ability or motives of my rivals. ____

To check your score and what it means, turn to page 211.

47 Implementation

Creativity can be defined as the ability to bring something into existence. The higher order of creativity is characterized by uniqueness and the convergent phases assure relevance. To complete the creative act, the ideas must be brought into existence in the real world. As Wallace Andrews remarked, "You can learn all you want about Freud, but sooner or later you have to go out with girls" (or boys, as the case may be). The efforts up to this point are meaningless unless the ideas are implemented to solve a problem.

Implementation does not just happen—it must be planned and managed.

> CONSTRUCT A STEP-BY-STEP PROGRAM SHOWING HOW YOU WOULD GO ABOUT IMPLEMENTING AN IDEA.

48 Innoways

In view of the obvious need for more creative thinking in all areas of living, and a rapidly growing interest toward creativity by large segments of our population, it is surprising to note that no one has, as yet, launched a publication or magazine that would be devoted to this subject matter, and that would have a wide popular appeal.

> ASSUME THAT YOU HAVE BEEN ASSIGNED THE PRO-JECT OF LAUNCHING A MAGAZINE CALLED *INNOWAYS*. LIST ALL POSSIBLE ARTICLES, COLUMNS, AND OTHER EDITORIAL MATERIAL SUCH A MAGA-ZINE COULD CONTAIN TO MAKE IT A SUCCESS.

49 20/10 Vision

For many centuries, the future has been a source of fear and uncertainty, as well as fascination. Speculating about it was left to astrologers, religious prophets, and some imaginative visionaries like Leonardo da Vinci, Charles Babbage, and Jules Verne.

Now the study of the future has become a formal discipline and thousands of people are involved, full-time, in the mapping of plausible alternative futures. Modern forecasting involves trend extrapolation, the Delphi technique, consensus scenarios, computer simulation, and various other techniques.

While these techniques help one to be more accurate in predictions, taking a look into the future is still dependent on the use of creative imagination. Studies have shown that not only are the creative managers more future-oriented, but that their forecasting abilities are well developed. Futurologists believe that people who are interested in the future tend to see more of it.

> WHAT DO YOU THINK LIES AHEAD IN BUSINESS AND TECHNOLOGY? FOCUSING ON THE YEAR 2010, WHAT SPECIFIC DEVELOPMENTS DO YOU FORESEE AS HAVING TAKEN PLACE, OR ABOUT TO HAPPEN?

50 Never Reject an Idea . . .

The image that most of us have of ourselves is that we are not only open-minded and willing to consider new ideas and proposals, but encouraging and supportive of them. Experience, however, has indicated that this attitude is seldom demonstrated in practice. As a matter of fact, most individuals have a hair-trigger tendency to be overly critical when evaluating a new idea. Their natural reaction to ideas is to look for the disadvantages in them, rather than for what is good in them.

> LET US ASSUME THAT YOU HAVE BEEN ASSIGNED THE TASK OF CHANGING THE OVERLY CRITICAL AND NEGATIVE ATTITUDES OF YOUR ORGANIZA- TION. AS THE FIRST STEP, YOU ARE TO ISSUE A LIST OF INJUNCTIONS, ALL STARTING WITH: NEVER RE- JECT AN IDEA BECAUSE . . .

Examples:

- Never reject an idea because you see something wrong with it.
- Never reject an idea because you won't get the credit.

Now it's your turn.

ANSWERS, POSSIBILITIES, AND ANALYSES

1   Test Your Creativity Quotient

SCORING

To compute your score, circle and add up the values assigned to each item.

	A	B	C
1.	0	1	2
2.	0	1	2
3.	4	1	0
4.	−2	0	3
5.	2	1	0
6.	−1	0	3
7.	3	0	−1

	A	B	C
8.	0	1	2
9.	3	0	−1
10.	1	0	3
11.	4	1	0
12.	3	0	−1
13.	2	1	0
14.	4	0	−2
15.	−1	0	2
16.	2	1	0
17.	0	1	2
18.	3	0	−1
19.	0	1	2
20.	0	1	2
21.	0	1	2
22.	3	0	−1
23.	0	1	2
24.	−1	0	2
25.	0	1	3
26.	−1	0	2
27.	2	1	0
28.	2	0	−1
29.	0	1	2
30.	−2	0	3
31.	0	1	2
32.	0	1	2
33.	3	0	−1
34.	−1	0	2
35.	0	1	2
36.	1	2	3
37.	2	1	0
38.	0	1	2
39.	−1	0	2

40. The following have values of 2:

energetic	dynamic	perceptive	dedicated
resourceful	flexible	innovative	courageous
original	observant	self-demanding	curious
enthusiastic	independent	persevering	involved

The following have values of 1:

self-confident	determined	informal	forward-looking
thorough	restless	alert	open-minded

The rest have values of 0.

WHAT YOUR SCORE MEANS

95–116	Exceptionally Creative
65–94	Very Creative
40–64	Above Average
20–39	Average
10–19	Below Average
Below 10	Noncreative

If you scored below your expectations, don't despair. By conscientiously doing the exercises and games in this book you can considerably enhance your creative powers.

· Keep track of your ideas at all times. Carry a notebook wherever you go, and keep it at your bedside. Ideas come at strange times, frequently when we least expect them, and they may never come again. Listen to your hunches and intuitions, particularly during moments of relaxation, before going to sleep, or upon awakening.

· Pose new questions every day. An inquiring mind is a creatively active mind. It is also a mind that constantly enlarges the area of its awareness.

· Learn about things outside of your specialty. Seemingly unrelated pieces of knowledge can often be brought together to solve problems or create new products and services.

· Avoid rigid, set patterns of doing things. Overcome fixed ideas and look for new viewpoints; try new ways. Attempt to find several solutions to each problem and develop the ability to drop one idea in favor of another.

· Be open and receptive to ideas, others' as well as yours. New ideas are fragile—listen positively to them. Seize on tentative, half-formed concepts and possibilities: A new idea seldom arrives as a complete ready-made package. Freely entertain apparently wild, farfetched, or even silly ideas.

· Be alert in observation. Look for similarities, differences, and unique and distinguishing features in objects, situations, processes, and ideas. The more new associations you can form, the greater are your chances of coming up with really original combinations and solutions.

· Engage in hobbies. Try ones that allow you to construct something with your hands. This allows you to relax and enhances the creative problem-solving abilities so useful in your work. Also, keep your brain trim by playing games and doing puzzles and exercises.

· Improve your sense of humor and laugh easily. This helps you to put yourself and your problems into proper perspective. Humor relieves tension, and you are more creative when you are relaxed.

· Adopt a risk-taking attitude. Nothing is more fatal to creativity than fear of failure.

2	Your Creative Achievements

It would be especially helpful if you could do this exercise with a group of people, each taking his or her turn to relate to the others the circumstances surrounding the achievement.

You can redo this exercise each time you experience inordinate difficulties with your present problems. It enables you to recapture and transfer the success associations and success sequences to what needs to be done.

<table>
<tr><td>**3**</td><td># Insights into Self</td></tr>
</table>

It is sometimes helpful to go over the future-oriented items: numbers 1, 4, 9, 18, 23, and 32. Note any recurrent or similar themes. These will reveal your most important aspirations. The other items that go to the core of your needs and values are numbers 3, 5, 10, 14, 20, 26, and 31. Review them for the light they can shed on them. Numbers 6, 7, 9, 17, 20, 26, 28, 29, 30, 31, and 33 through 50 will give you important insights into your work situation and how you react to environmental happenings.

<table>
<tr><td>**4**</td><td># Crystallizing Your Values and Increasing Self-Understanding</td></tr>
</table>

Sometimes when you examine your past priorities in the light of your new, crystallized value system, you may discover that many of your previous concerns are no longer meaningful. This discovery alone can be a giant step toward career success. Frequently you will find that you have either outgrown or radically modified your old priorities. For example, you may discover that your present career—no matter the extent of your success—is not providing the psychological income you really need, or is not offering the new opportunities for which you are now ready. These kinds of discoveries may have a profound effect on your life, so be prepared.

In this rapidly changing world, each one of us needs to reexamine our values and priorities. Self-scrutiny that leads to a crystallized value system gives us a clearer idea of what we really want out of life and what new objectives would be most satisfying for us to pursue. We will begin to see the real world more realistically and learn to recognize demands that conflict with our basic priorities.

ANALYSIS OF VALUES CLARIFICATION

7–10 High discrepancy scores indicate that these are your primary areas of concern.

4–6 Moderate discrepancy scores show some concern with these values; you should probably also strive to address them.

0–3 Low discrepancy scores indicate that you are relatively happy with their realization.

PERSONALITY NEEDS—AND ANALYSIS

A. Add up the values for questions 1, 13, 17, 28, 33, 44, 52 ____
B. Add up the values for questions 2, 14, 18, 27, 34, 43, 51 ____
C. Add up the values for questions 3, 15, 19, 26, 35, 42, 50 ____
D. Add up the values for questions 4, 16, 20, 25, 36, 41, 49 ____
E. Add up the values for questions 5, 9, 24, 32, 40, 45, 56 ____
F. Add up the values for questions 6, 10, 23, 31, 39, 46, 55 ____
G. Add up the values for questions 7, 11, 22, 30, 38, 47, 54 ____
H. Add up the values for questions 8, 12, 21, 29, 37, 48, 53 ____

Note in which categories you put the highest scores. A high score in category A indicates that you place a high premium on achievement and recognition. A high score in category B shows that you enjoy taking dominance and leadership positions in social situations. A high score in category C means that assertiveness/ aggressiveness is your strong personality need. A high score in D demonstrates traits of exhibitionism and self-aggrandizement. A high score in category E means that your needs for belongingness and loyalty are predominant. A high score in F indicates a strong need for conformity and adaptation. A high score in category G shows that your basic needs are for order and predictability. A high score in H shows that you place a high premium on security.

Count the number of times you answered "yes" and the number of times you answered "no." If you responded "yes" more often than "no," your self-esteem is in good shape. Countless experiments and case studies have shown a high positive correlation between success and a healthy level of self-esteem. If you responded "no" more frequently, remember that your score is not immutably established for the rest of your life. You can develop more positive attitudes about yourself by merely starting to behave in a more self-assertive and self-confident manner.

5 Building Your Skills Profile

Analyze those skills that you have ranked most important. Which skills do you need to improve and what new skills do you need to acquire?

In planning to improve or acquire skills, keep these questions in mind:

- Who could I contact to learn more specifically how I could improve this skill?
- Who do I know who has this particular skill? How could I learn from this person?
- What books would be helpful?
- Are there any courses or training programs I could take?
- What new experiences would help me with this skill?
- What opportunities could I seek to practice this skill?
- How can I overcome any barriers?

6 The Possible Dream

One of the reasons people fail to realize their dreams is that they did not pick the "right" dreams in the first place. The right dreams are not simply the dreams that are the most desirable. They are the ones that are most consistent with a person's values, personality, and activities and are most deeply significant for that person. Because the objectives we really want to reach in life are frequently subjugated to the dictates and demands of our immediate environment and circumstances, it is helpful to periodically redo the inventory.

7 Visualizing Your Goals

Visualization is a technique not only for attaining specific organizational goals. You can use it to create a day-to-day life more in harmony with your deepest desires and values. It allows you to gain more control over your world and to shape your daily life into something more enjoyable and exciting. Visualization can be used effectively in all areas of living.

8 | Fear of Failure

SCORING INSTRUCTIONS

To get your score for the test, circle and add up the values for items 1 through 25.

ITEM	ANSWERS		
	A	**B**	**C**
1.	−2	1	2
2.	1	0	−1
3.	3	1	−2
4.	−1	0	1
5.	−2	0	2
6.	3	0	−2
7.	2	1	−1
8.	−2	1	2
9.	−2	0	2
10.	2	1	−1
11.	−2	0	2
12.	−2	1	2
13.	3	0	−3
14.	2	0	−2
15.	−2	0	2
16.	0	1	2
17.	2	1	−1
18.	3	0	−2
19.	3	0	−2
20.	−1	0	1
21.	−2	0	1
22.	−2	0	2
23.	3	0	−2
24.	−3	0	3
25.	−3	0	3

WHAT YOUR SCORE MEANS

35 to 54 You're seldom preoccupied with the possibility of failure. Rather, you move toward your objectives with a sure feeling of confidence and act as if it is impossible for you to fail. You have the ability to stick with difficult tasks and problems and you seldom give up. You seldom compare your achievements with others', but if you do, you almost always feel you could have done better than they did. Attributes of self-reliance and self-trust enable you to remain imperturbable in many challenging situations. You're able to maintain continuous drive and a high level of thrust in whatever you do.

8 to 34 You're occasionally hampered by an overly cautious and hesitant attitude toward your objectives. Frequently you even entertain serious doubts about reaching the goals you've set for yourself. You have trouble concentrating when something important is at stake. Before you act on your ideas, you feel compelled to enlist other managers' opinions and evaluations of your plans. If they don't approve or encourage you, you frequently give up on your plans.

−25 to 8 A marked fear of failure in many areas is indicated. You lack self-trust and have an unrealistically low image of yourself. You tend to eschew important tasks and busy yourself with the tried and true. Competitive situations are anathema for you, as is being with people you don't know. In meetings you feel that everyone else has more witty and knowledgeable things to say than you do. Because of your fear of failure, your aspirations are low and you hesitate to take any kind of risks.

−45 to −24 You show complete lack of confidence and you're constantly worried about your capabilities. You avoid any and all challenges and prefer to stick with routine, familiar tasks. With other people you seek timid accommodation and dislike people who show boisterous self-assertion. Because you fear failure so much, you have antisuccess attitudes and feel that those managers who climb the ladder of success will find upon reaching the top that it isn't resting on anything.

9 | Other Uses

POSSIBILITIES

1. For decoration (shoes, handbags, etc.).   2. As play money.   3. To draw circles.   4. Make necklace.
5. Make earrings   6. As poker chips.   7. Means of exchange.   8. Make pictures.   9. Stop up sink.
10. Teach children how to count.   11. Collect as a hobby.   12. Practice sewing.   13. To throw at people.   14. In lieu of checkers.   15. Use in bingo.
16. Make rattles.   17. As noses for dolls.   18. Sell to developing countries.   19. Make eyes on dolls, animals, snowmen, etc.   20. Use as a slug.   21. Use as a small target.   22. To suck or chew on.   23. As a play monocle.   24. Make bracelet.   25. Play with when nervous.   26. Hide tear or spot on dress.   27. Hide a hole in a wall.   28. Advertise for office in election.   29. Pry open cans, jars, etc.   30. Use as paperweight.   31. Swing from a swing to scare flies.   32. Use as pressure object to stop bleeding.   33. Use as golf marker.   34. A map marker.
35. Construct a pendulum.   36. Flip as a coin.   37. Hold name tag.   38. Christmas tree decoration.   39. Teach handicapped children self-help.   40. Sift bread crumbs through holes.   41. Stuff dolls.   42. Stuff a bean bag.   43. Hang from string to see where the wind blows.   44. Swallow to get sick.   45. Put in fish pond.   46. At end of string attached to light.   47. Play catch with.   48. Wheels of a toy car.
49. Make knob on lid.   50. Put on string for cat to play with.

10 Verbal Dexterity I

Part One: Tight. Smart. Double. Wise.
Part Two: Topaz. Opal. Garnet.
Part Three: Strike. String. Go. Dry. Dress.
Dog. Body.
Part Four: Each word contains part of the head or body.
Part Five: ON. ER. SP. PE. AL.
Part Six: Harmony. Happy. Happen. Harvest.
Have. Hazard. Help. High. Hide.

11 Peripatetic Women

POSSIBILITIES

- Women don't want to play organizational politics and hence get bypassed by promotions. As a result they look for other jobs.
- They know that to advance rapidly these days one has to change jobs often.
- They follow their spouses' job changes and with sequential marriages this leads to frequent turnover.
- They consider office work alienating and are always looking for greener pastures.
- They get fed up with the salary differential between them and men for the same type of work, and are looking for jobs where fairer pay practices prevail.
- They enter the job market to hunt for husbands and change jobs often to find "the right one."
- They are multitalented with a wide range of interests and

are looking for jobs where these talents and interests would be fully utilized.
- They cannot handle pressure and stress well and are looking for more relaxed organizations to work for.
- They are not listened to by male bosses and are looking to work for female bosses.
- They don't know what they really want and are unrealistic in their job aspirations.

12 | Suggestion Systems

POSSIBILITIES

1. Present a citation in the form of a certificate or plaque to each major winner.
2. Run pictures and biographical sketches of employees whose suggestions are used in in-house publications.
3. Periodically publicize suggestions previously adopted.
4. Publish a monthly list of employees who win awards for suggestions.
5. Provide some form of recognition to employees whose ideas are *not* adopted.
6. Stress management's desire for specific types of suggestions through periodic company announcements.
7. Introduce a serial feature called "Win with Ideas," outlining some ten problems in each issue.
8. Request various departments to formulate specific problems in need of solutions.
9. Form "idea circles." Require a definite number of suggestions or qualifications for joining.
10. Assure employees that there will be no layoffs as a result of any suggestion adopted.
11. Inform those whose suggestions were good why they were *not* adopted.
12. Publish pictures and stories about employees who continuously submit a large number of ideas.

13. Give premiums of merchandise for good ideas.
14. Have a stock option or profit-sharing plan for profitable ideas.
15. Establish an "Ideator of the Year" award for the employee who submits the most and best suggestions.
16. Show pictorially "before and after" effects of ideas that were adopted.
17. Publish articles explaining techniques involved in thinking up ideas.
18. Publish a feature story on the company's patent department.
19. Publish an annual report on how much money was made, or saved, through suggestions that were implemented.
20. Conduct workshop seminars on creative problem solving.
21. Have the company CEO write to each employee who submits a usable idea.
22. Hold a banquet for people who submitted ideas.
23. Establish committees comprised of all strata of the company to judge the usability of ideas.
24. Conduct idea contests with prizes for quality ideas.
25. Publish stories tracing the origins of ideas that were accepted.
26. Make qualified professionals and specialists available for assistance to employees who want to develop ideas.
27. Show how an idea mushrooms into an improved working climate for everybody.
28. Feature stories about those who gained promotions by offering usable ideas.
29. Explain how new ideas improve the company's competitive posture.
30. Show how job security is enhanced by usable suggestions.

13 Like/Unlike

SYNONYMS	ANTONYMS
1. reject	1. dash
2. rational	2. durable
3. regard	3. decide
4. radiant	4. discover
5. reasonable	5. diversity
6. calling	6. magnify
7. cite	7. massive
8. calamity	8. miserly
9. consequence	9. manifest
10. compute	10. miss
11. harmony	11. perfect
12. habitual	12. perpetuate
13. hoax	13. peaceful
14. harmless	14. palatable
15. haggle	15. positive

14 What Could It Be?

POSSIBILITIES

Hot-mobile: hot-dog vendor's cart, an elephant's breath, a lighted cigar being thrown into a trash can.

Cold-silvery: coins on a cold day, someone wearing a silver ring putting their hand in a freezer, an outdoor thermometer during the winter.

Large-wooden: a tree, a building, a wooden sculpture, a wooden bridge.

Small-metallic: a dime, a paper clip, a thumbtack.

Fast-electrical: a high-speed train, a neon light, a watch, a clothes iron falling out of a window.

Slow-glass: marbles used by someone with only two fingers, windows on a car stalled in heavy traffic.

Square-slippery: a newly waxed floor tile, a wet sidewalk, a block of ice.

Round-rough: a used croquet ball, a porcupine in the fetal position, a man with a crew cut and an unshaven face.

Expensive-transparent: a diamond, crystal stemware, gasoline.

Inexpensive-flexible: rubber bands, straws, taffy, chewing gum.

---

15 | Odd One Out

ANSWERS

1. meter
2. temper
3. shorts
4. lavender
5. France
6. nicotine
7. contradiction
8. Indians
9. tennis
10. courage
11. moon
12. thirty
13. weaken
14. pine
15. stroke
16. highway
17. hockey
18. wool
19. coral
20. Monte Carlo

16 | Are You Intuitive?

SCORING AND ANALYSIS

If you correctly answered nine to twelve you tend to place a high value on intuition. As a consequence, you find your greatest satisfaction when dealing with new ideas, new possibilities and directions, rather than what already exists. Your intuitive bent leads you to approach problems in a novel and fresh manner.

A score of five to eight indicates that you're flexible and effective in both the world of new ideas and when implementing well-thought-out plans and procedures. Even though you believe in your hunches, you tend to subject them to systematic and critical scrutiny.

A score of zero to four shows that you're strongly analytical and objectively critical. You tend to value clear reasoning and logic, and are suspicious of any intuitive promptings, unless they can be subjected to thorough analysis and demonstrable proof.

1. I think that, other things being equal, a logical, step-by-step method is still the best way for solving problems. **False.** Only very simple problems call for thinking in which rational sequences unfold in a straight and predictable line. Most problems over the full range of business situations are as convoluted as the folds on the surface of the human brain. The creative or intuitive manager is flexible and able to choose a wide variety of approaches to his problem, without losing sight of his overall goal. He can easily drop one line of thought and take up another, change perspectives, and discard one frame of reference for another. He is able to perceive a problem from different viewpoints and he prefers to consider many ideas before deciding on one to solve his problem.

2. Good hunches have provided the impetus for many of my successful projects. **True.** Success for many managers who frequently have to make decisions on the basis of incomplete information depends to a large extent on their capacity for coming up with good hunches. It is their ability to arrive at correct hunches combined with a willingness to take risks that determine the success of their projects.

3. I have lived to regret many of my actions and decisions that went counter to my intuitive feelings. **True.** Many intuitive managers have reported that whenever they have acted contrary to their intuitive feelings—either through outside coercion, or merely because they distrusted their hunches—the outcomes have been disappointing.

4. In order for me to act upon a decision, it has to "feel right." **True.** Although a decision may look sound and logical, it may not be translated into effective action because certain contingencies were overlooked. One of the basic attributes of the effective decision maker is his ability to select among many alternatives the best course of action, or the one that "feels right," even though none of them is a sure bet.

5. In my experience, intuitive hunches have proven to be unreliable guides to action. **False.** Genuine intuitive hunches are reliable in that they enable one to sense the as-yet-not-realized possibilities inherent in a situation. If an apparently intuitive perception turns out to be wrong, it did not emerge from intuition, but from self-deception or wishful thinking.

6. I feel that many of my ideas seem to grow out of their own roots, as if independent of my will. **True.** These moments of rare intensity, when everything falls easily into place and a new idea is born, or a problem solved, has been reported by almost every creative manager, no matter what his field. So spontaneous and uncontrived is this process that he has the impression that the ideas came from without.

7. I have very little interest in problems that do not have clear-cut answers. **False.** One significant reason for the lack of ability to produce new ideas among many managers is their strong preference for precise and clear thoughts, and their tendency to reject problems that are too intangible to permit immediate comprehension. Creative managers are not only tolerant of ambiguity, but actively seek out complex and challenging problems. As a result, they are more aware of the intricate and paradoxical qualities in many problem situations.

8. I regard myself as unconventional, independent and spontaneous, and I enjoy taking risks. **True.** In psychological testing situations creative managers tend to describe themselves in these terms. They further report that they are not afraid of ambiguities or uncertainties and are willing to expose themselves to challenge.

9. I have the ability to penetrate to the essence of a situa-

tion. **True.** A genuine intuitive feeling helps a manager to penetrate the complex interplay of elements he is dealing with to the very crux of the situation. Without this intuitive feeling he is apt to get lost in a welter of irrelevant issues and miss the central point of the problem.

10. When I get a hunch, I feel compelled to act on it. **True.** An intuitive hunch is often accompanied by a sense of compulsion that urges the manager to do something about it immediately, even though the time or occasion for action may not always be propitious.

11. I tend to rely on the feeling of "rightness" or "wrongness" when moving toward the solution of a problem. **True.** For creative managers the problem-solving process is held together by feeling. They trust their feelings for telling them what belongs and what does not belong. They have the capacity to feel the direction of a possible solution for their problem before they actually know what the solution is.

12. Many of the penetrating insights I have experienced have been touched off by seemingly insignificant coincidences. **True.** Penetrating insights usually occur at the culminating point of a long series of commonly unnoticed, or subconscious, insights. What slowly, and perhaps unbeknownst to the manager, has been germinating and going forward, comes suddenly into full view as a result of an externally perceived coincidence. Although insight is essentially a function of inner processes and not of outer circumstances, the telescoping of a cluster of insights into one major insight is frequently triggered by outside occurrences.

17 | Taking Charge of Your Time

Prioritization and planning your projects in a methodical way are extremely important, for they free you up and move you toward a more effective use of your time. As someone has put it, "Efficiency is doing things right. Effectiveness is doing the right things." Priorities should be based on the expected outcomes of the use of time and energy and the overall benefit expected from investing time in each task you tackle. Allocate ample time for highest priorities. Do first things first and stick to your priorities. However, your daily schedule should allow room for unanticipated developments, restraints and demands that you need to attend to. If you don't allow for unanticipated developments you may not be able to complete planned activities within the time you allotted for them. By recognizing that certain unexpected demands and restraints will occur, you can moderate their adverse effects on the time you allotted for important tasks.

Each day make a list of the following day's tasks and activities. A written list allows you to schedule, space, and control your time. Your list should include tasks you *must* complete, things you should get done, and things that *could* be done. Allocate prime working time to your "must do" list.

Make sure that your "must do" list includes *important* creative projects and not just *urgent* ones. Some managers are so intent on just tackling urgent duties that they don't allocate enough time for creative but not urgent tasks.

Beware of time-wasting "busy work." Many of our daily tasks fall into this category of activities that are neither urgent nor important, but somehow diversionary. They provide an illusion of activity and accomplishment and serve as an excuse to postpone action on important objectives.

Here are some examples you can use to construct a more effective time management program for yourself:

- Block out time each day for the currently most important objective and do not permit any interruptions.
- Save your "prime time"—that period every day when you work at your peak performance—for this important objective.
- Make every effort to handle any kind of document or paper only once. While it is in your hand, do something about it.
- Answer most correspondence on the letters themselves, as they are read.
- Avoid rewriting and try to get it right the first time. You'll concentrate better if you know you're not going to revise it.
- Learn to say no to unreasonable demands.
- Don't let others dump their time-wasting activities on you.

- Delegate jobs, travel, attending meetings, writing reports to subordinates, if it can be done.
- Make use of time spent waiting for appointments. Carry reading material with you.
- Group tasks that fit together, e.g. telephone calls.
- Procrastinate deliberately on useless tasks. Ask yourself the question, "What if I don't do this at all?"
- Try to anticipate and avoid unnecessary interruptions. If possible, isolate yourself when you need uninterrupted time for creative thinking, or start your day early.
- Discourage unnecessary interruptions. Remember, if you don't act as if your time is valuable, neither will anyone else. Show others that you prize your time and theirs. When someone interrupts you, say you'll get back to them later. Set aside a time when people can see you, and don't see anyone at other times.
- Resist the urge to discuss. Many things can be expeditiously dispatched with a few written words via memos, short notes, and marginal comments.
- Listen carefully and actively in order to get the other person's message the first time.
- Concentrate on one job at a time. If you work on one task and worry about another, neither will be accomplished satisfactorily.
- Do complex tasks in two-hour blocks. Allow no interruptions during this time.
- C. Northcote Parkinson's law says that "work expands in direct relation to the time available for its completion." If you allow yourself four hours to complete a task, it will take that long. If you only allow two hours, chances are you'll accomplish it in that amount of time. Often we waste time unconsciously.
- Although it might be impossible to eliminate all routine, ask why something is "always done that way." Consider ways to eliminate the unnecessary and still obtain the same results by altering procedures.
- On certain activities you can use a timer to limit time use.
- If possible, avoid long luncheons.
- Don't let procrastination, regrets, frustrations, or anxiety steal your time away.
- Use commuting, waiting, dressing, bathing, etc. time doing

147

your planning and thinking; have a notebook at hand to write down ideas you consider significant. If you drive, use the time for dictating or for learning from cassette tapes.

- Eliminate or cut down on small time-wasters: watching TV programs you don't enjoy, conversing with people who bore you, doing chores you can put off, etc.
- Plan your next day's activities at a regular time each day. Decide on most important tasks.
- At the end of each day note ways in which you have wasted time.
- Review your task lists periodically for patterns. Analyze the patterns honestly. What were the really necessary and useful activities? What could have been eliminated? What were the frills? Are you too often busy with urgent things to the detriment of important things? Are you devoting too much time to objectives that are not really important?
- Determine the specific tasks and activities you could eliminate totally to have more time for pursuing creative objectives. Become aware of the things that you do that deplete you of energy. Which of these could you drop to make your time more productive and valuable?
- Analyze how you could reorganize your time, both at work and at home, to utilize it to best advantage.

Some of the biggest time-consumers are paperwork, meetings, and telephone conversations. Here are some time-saving ideas for these three areas:

PAPERWORK

- Don't read your mail until you plan to take action on each piece requiring a response.
- Classify letters to be written or dictated.
- Put all second- and third-class mail aside, to be skimmed later.
- Read selectively and skim over unimportant matters.
- After sorting papers and documents, handle each of them only once.
- Send time-limit response memos.
- Abbreviate where possible.

148

- Delegate papers to someone else.
- File notes where you can readily find them.
- Set up an in-basket system according to priorities.

MEETINGS

- Don't call a meeting when you can handle it by phone.
- Set up luncheon meetings with everyone at the same time.
- Hold informal meetings standing up.
- Hold formal meetings close to the lunch break or late in the afternoon.
- Stick to designated start and end times for all meetings.
- Distribute premeeting agendas and notes. Ask everyone to come prepared for decisions/actions.
- Meet in a place other than your office so you can leave on time.
- Hold meetings in a place where you won't be interrupted.
- Ask for clarification of issues when discussion wanders.
- Don't hesitate to terminate useless discussions.
- Expect meetings to end with an action plan.

TELEPHONE

- Schedule specific times at which you will be available to receive calls.
- Jot down points you want to make before you make a call.
- Keep calls brief and businesslike.
- Speak to someone else if called party is unavailable.
- Make calls when you are most likely to contact your party.
- Don't wait excessively on the phone.
- Train your secretary or someone else to handle many of your calls for you.
- Send a wire or memo if you have trouble getting a specific party.

18 | Are You Under the Right Amount of Stress?

SCORING

Add up your points based on the answer key below.

	OFTEN	SOME-TIMES	SELDOM	NEVER
1.	7	4	1	0
2.	7	4	1	0
3.	6	3	1	0
4.	4	2	0	0
5.	7	3	1	0
6.	6	3	1	0
7.	6	3	1	0
8.	5	2	0	0
9.	7	3	1	0
10.	4	2	0	0
11.	4	2	0	0
12.	4	2	0	0
13.	4	2	0	0
14.	4	2	0	0
15.	4	2	0	0
16.	6	4	1	0

	YES	NO
17.	4	0
18.	0	3
19.	0	4
20.	0	5
21.	0	5
22.	3	0
23.	4	0
24.	0	3
25.	5	0

	YES	NO
26.	4	0
27.	0	3
28.	0	3
29.	0	3
30.	4	0
31.	3	0
32.	6	0
33.	3	0
34.	4	0
35.	3	0
36.	0	3
37.	0	3
38.	0	4

WHAT YOUR SCORE MEANS

70–167 A score in this range not only indicates that your problems seem to outnumber your satisfactions, but that you're presently subjected to a high level of stress. You're no doubt already aware of your myriad unwellness, and you're rightfully concerned about your own psychological and physical well-being.

By all means, you should do everything possible to avoid as many stressful situations as you can until you feel more in control of your life. It might be a good idea for you to go over the quiz to pinpoint the major sources or events of your present stress.

You might also need to develop more effective ways to manage your responses to stressful situations. Your vulnerability to stressful events shows that you are perhaps overreacting to problems, or it may be that you're not as willing to cope creatively with adversities as you could be. You might want to consider seeking professional help. Sometimes even a few hours of counseling can be of great help. You might also want to pay heed to the wise words of a cardiologist who offers the following three rules for combating stress: 1. Don't sweat the small stuff. 2. Everything is small stuff. 3. If you can't fight it, or flee from it, flow with it.

45–69 A score spanning this range either indicates that your stress seems to be moderate, or that you're probably handling your frustrations quite well. You should, however, review various aspects of your daily work and life and try to relieve stress before it starts building up. Because you seem to have occasional difficulties coping with the effects of stress, you might want to consider adding some new methods of dealing with disappointments. Remember, we all have to face and live with occasional states of unwellness; we can even ignore them, or we can turn situations of stress and pressure into an opportunity for further creative growth. The choice is largely ours.

0–44 A score in this range indicates that your stress is relatively low and you're probably in great shape. In spite of minor worries and concerns, stress doesn't seem to be causing you any serious problems.

You have, no doubt, good adaptive powers and are able to deal quite well with situations that make you, temporarily, uptight. You seem to have been able to strike a good balance in your ability to cope with and control stress.

CHRONIC FATIGUE

One serious consequence of stress is chronic fatigue. The manager who experiences this is half-bushed even before he gets to work, and exhausted by the time he should be at his peak.

The following suggestions might help you to get the most out of your day's work:

1. At the office, take a breather when you start becoming irritable. This is the first sign of approaching fatigue. Short breaks are probably more refreshing than long rests. A too-lengthy rest period may actually decrease creative efficiency, since the longer you are away from your job the more energy you have to expend in "warming up" to it later on.

2. If you feel habitually and inexplicably tired week after week, look first for a physical reason. See your doctor for a thorough checkup. Poor vision alone may cause your fatigue, so check your eyesight. If you are dieting, plan a slower reducing program.

3. Try resting and sleeping more, if you believe your fatigue is merely due to work. If that does not do the trick, you must look to your emotions.

4. Check your posture. Notice that when you slump in your chair and let your head droop, you feel listless; straighten your back, hold your head up and you're no longer listless. In other words, act energetic and chances are you may soon feel energetic.

5. Exercise is a valuable antidote to fatigue. After an exhausting day, a little exercise can work wonders.

6. Stop racing and start looking where you're going. A major cause of nerve and brain exhaustion is our modern rush-rush-rush way of living. Rather than promoting pep, hurrying really tends to reduce your energy.

7. Use your sense of humor to fight tiredness. If you cannot sleep off fatigue, sometimes you can laugh it off.

CAUSES OF EXCESSIVE STRESS

What causes excessive stress? Any number of things can be at the root of unpleasant stress—meeting impossible deadlines, making important decisions, personality conflicts with associates, excessive responsibility, fear of failure, fear of criticism, excessive ambition, business reversals, and many other factors.

Work addiction can also produce stress and there are many managers who are workaholics. They have either become this way because of their personalities, or because a shortage of creative associates has put a taxing load of work on their shoulders. They act as if their reservoirs of mental and physical energy were inexhaustible.

Unfortunately, every person has a breaking point when subjected to excessive stress, and everyone reaches a stage, usually well before breakdown, at which continuing stress produces a major loss of efficiency.

One's own attitude can aggravate the situation. It is a good idea to stop occasionally and confront onself with these questions: Are matters really as urgent as they seem? What would happen if the deadline on this project were shifted ahead a week or so? Impatience and inflexible adherence to deadlines, which may have been set unrealistically in the first place, create much harmful stress.

One good way to eliminate job-related stress is to analyze your job. Instead of going off in a dozen different directions, structure your tasks. List the things you have to do and organize them according to priority, with most urgent tasks topping the list. Then, as you complete each task, stress will ease up and the feeling of being overwhelmed will vanish.

Stress can also be touched off by conditions outside the job situation and then simply spill over into the job. Many managers tend to blame their stress on excessive pressures and business conditions. While this is often true, many remain oblivious to the fact that their habitual behavior patterns after working hours weaken their ability to cope even with mildly stressful situations on the job. It is well known that many managers do not get enough exercise—they prefer to ride or drive rather than walk. Lack of exercise and the ready availability of food and drink create a weight problem. The passive entertainment that TV provides removes the lively and nourishing stimulus that conversation and creative games and hobbies provide. Not having recharged their batteries during their leisure hours, is it any wonder that problems at work tend to be magnified out of all proportion?

HOW TO PREVENT OR COMBAT STRESS

There are a great many things managers can do to prevent or combat excessive stress. Here's a partial listing:

1. Reduce the overtime you put in, either at work or at home.

2. Leave your briefcase at work, if at all possible.

3. Become aware of the limits of your permissible stress.

4. Get up from your chair at least once every two hours and walk about for a few minutes.

5. Take a breather now and then. Stand up; inhale deeply and deliberately and let your breath out slowly.

6. Slump in your seat from time to time and relax all your muscles.

7. Stretch hard. Roll your shoulders and head, windmill your arms. Flop your hands vigorously at the wrists.

8. Inject a change into your routine. Go to a different restaurant for lunch; walk instead of ride to the station.

9. Sit back occasionally and analyze your job objectively and detachedly. New perspectives frequently alleviate the pressures.

10. Have friends over to your home at least once a week.

11. Spend at least two evenings a week enjoying a creative hobby.

12. If you've lost recreational time, be sure to make up for this.

13. Find out the root cause of your present fatigue. If excessively fatigued day after day, you may find that more physical activity might relieve it.

14. Relaxation in small doses is an effective antidote to excessive stress. This does not always mean rest. More often than not, it

means a change of scene, a change of activity, an "upsetting of the needle in the groove."

15. One of the best cures for stress fatigue is exercise, and the easiest and frequently the best exercise is walking.

16. Learn to handle your emotions constructively.

17. Recognize and heed your personal danger signals.

18. Make use of your built-in shock absorbers. Rationalize away certain anxieties; suppress problems you can do nothing about. These are legitimate mental mechanisms we all use in our daily self-therapy.

---

19 | Match Point

ANSWERS

1. $$IV + I = V$$

2. $$II - I = I$$

3. $$III + II = V$$

4. $$V + IV = IX$$

$$VI + IV = X$$

5.

6.

$$V - IV = V\sqrt{}$$

7.

NIL

8.

IX I=I

---

20 | Coping with Neophobia

THE FALSE SECURITY OF THE FAMILIAR

Time-tested methods, standard procedures, policies, and rules give many individuals a feeling of security. The clearly defined, the firmly established, the things that make their world secure and predictable, have a powerful hold on them. A proposed new idea thus frequently appears as a direct threat to their sense of security. "After all," the reasoning goes, "why should we disturb things as they are when they seem to be working well?"

There is also a feeling that accepting a new idea may denigrate the validity of what exists. Or the reasoning goes, "We have enough problems as it is, why add problems we might not even be able to cope with?" Clearly, accepting change, which new ideas inevitably brings about, means more headaches, work, and responsibility.

This clinging to the status quo would be all right, of course, if things stayed put, and if it were not for the fact that there exist companies which encourage new ideas and bold creative advances and thus move ahead by leaps and bounds. It has been observed that companies whose management fears innovation develop into copiers, or seek only relatively small, predictable, and orderly improvements. The danger in this unrealistic caution and the tendency to cling to the familiar is that it may stunt the creative growth of the organization to a degree where it fails to adequately cope with competition.

NEW IDEAS THREATEN SECURITY AND STATUS

Some people react negatively to a new idea because it is not their own. Many managers are especially prone to play down the value of new ideas because they feel that their power and status are threatened if their underlings or even their associates suggest them. They resist ideas because they were not the first to think of them.

Change is also frequently fought because it makes someone's job insecure, or tumbles an expert from his pinnacle. For example, a technical innovation may introduce a completely new approach with which a particular job is tackled. A man who for years has followed a particular practice with great skill and confidence may suddenly find himself a novice who is feeling his way and who is starting the slow, painful path of learning a new skill.

Innovative change may undermine individuals' security in other ways than just loss of status or skill. It may also be perceived as a direct threat to their earnings, position, chance for advancement, recognition, and favorable working conditions.

TRANSGRESSION INTO PRIVATE DOMAINS

Some people feel that new ideas, especially when they originate in another department of the company, encroach on their rightful province. Each person's responsibility in organizations is, as a rule, carefully defined. When somebody comes up with an idea that concerns some other person's area, the usual reaction is defensiveness and/or hostility, for the person tends to feel that nobody else has the right to trespass into his area of specialization.

WHEN DO PEOPLE RESENT CHANGE MOST?

Here is a summary of recent research findings on why people resent change. They resent change:

· When the purpose of the proposed change is not spelled out clearly. Ambiguity can trigger anxiety, unrest, and fear. And experience has shown that fear of change can be more disrupting than the change itself.

· When employees are not involved, or have not been asked to participate in the planning and implementation of the proposed change. They are apt to cooperate more readily when they are asked to help in solving problems that affect them. They tend to support what they have helped to create.

· When they are exhorted to have or show their loyalty to the company. Loyalty is a desirable attitude, but it cannot be elicited by management edict, and it alone is insufficient for people to accept change. Only specific knowledge of how the change will get something done is legitimately persuasive.

· When a radical modification in the group's habit patterns and the network of working relationships is proposed.

· When communication regarding the change is channeled only to a few. Even though a change may affect only a few people in a department, to maintain team cohesiveness, cooperation, and the feeling of security everybody needs to be informed.

· When change threatens to augment present workloads excessively.

· When the explicit and implicit rewards for making the change are seen to be inadequate.

Change can be introduced best when:

· Individuals are asked to participate in the planning and implementation stages of the proposed change. This helps them to understand what the change is all about and gives them confidence that management is genuinely interested in utilizing their ideas and suggestions.

· Employees are allowed, or even encouraged, to freely air their resistance and objections to a proposed change. Sometimes these are valid and sound reactions. Even if some of their objections are unrealistic or not well thought through, the airing of grievances has a cathartic value and frequently reduces the initial resistance.

· Communications regarding a proposed change are complete

and adequate. Employees know the reasons for the change and what it will accomplish. Inadequate or incomplete communication builds mistrust. Even if the change involves something that is not altogether pleasant, employees would rather have the bad news than no news at all. In one case, a company was threatened with bankruptcy because it wouldn't lower the price and compete with a similar product made in Japan. Top management let everybody know the facts. Employees were able to suggest several innovative cost-cutting procedures which were adopted. The result was increased productivity. The company not only got back on its feet, but is flourishing today.

REALISTIC RESISTANCE TO NEW IDEAS

It should be pointed out that there are sometimes valid and compelling reasons for the rejection of new ideas.

Occasionally the sheer number of ongoing projects is so large that undertaking work on new ideas might disrupt the work the company is already committed to accomplish. In this case it is obvious that the idea is one whose time has not yet come, and it should be held in abeyance until a more propitious occasion.

Occasionally a good idea would be so costly to develop that it would be impracticable to undertake from the company's standpoint. Simple economics in most companies dictates what can and what cannot be developed.

Sometimes a new idea involves only a small part of a procedure that is scheduled for a complete change. The proposed partial idea may not fit in with the planned overall change.

There are also occasionally quite legitimate reasons why a person should refrain from putting in the extra time and effort involved in developing a presentation for his idea. His regular duties might be such that he has little time to devote to the task. Or his idea might be in an area where his background knowledge or existing information that would buttress his sales argument is either incomplete or unavailable. Why risk one's good reputation for sound judgment by being forced to admit this publicly?

21 | Smugnosis

POSSIBILITIES

1. We don't do it that way in our company.
2. It costs too much.
3. Our business is different.
4. We'll come back to it later.
5. It's not practical
6. It leaves me cold.
7. Let's think about it some more.
8. Let someone else try it first.
9. The market won't hold still for that.
10. It's not in the manual.
11. You don't seem to understand the problem.
12. The boss will never accept it.
13. It will increase overhead.
14. We've never used that technique before.
15. This is political dynamite in our company.
16. It won't work in our industry.
17. Why something new now? Our profits are still going up.
18. Customers won't accept it.
19. That's not our department's problem.
20. We have too many projects now.
21. It's not in the budget.

22 | Decisions, Decisions

Examples of some of the major barriers that interfere with effective decision making include:

· *The notion of first solution.* Many managers have the tendency to grab the first solution that comes to their minds. Yet, countless experiments have shown that first solutions rarely, if ever, are the best. Defer consideration of first solutions. Marshal as many alternative solutions to your problem as possible.

· *The notion of previous success.* It is a fallacy to believe that because a solution worked on a previous problem, it will work on the present problem. Problems can look similar on the surface, but closer analysis can reveal basic differences.

· *The notion of unalterable consequences.* A decision reduces the number of alternatives subsequently available. But it does not eliminate them completely. A decision is not like a train, which, once in motion, must continue on a given track. Quite the contrary. Even after the wheels have begun to turn there are still many opportunities to alter the decision and therefore the consequences of the decision.

· *The notion of finality.* Related to the above is the fallacy that once a decision has been made, one can't change it. Many managers feel that reversing or changing a decision, especially when it has been communicated to others, may imply faulty planning, inefficiency, or lack of analytical ability. Some managers find it impossible to admit, even to themselves, that they've made a faulty decision.

Sometimes a decision can be sound at the time it is made. But changing circumstances or the uncovering of new information may dictate modification or reversal of the original decision. Sticking to a wrong decision may work for awhile. But the eventual repercussions could be much worse than modifying a decision that looks like a poor bet.

· *The notion of committee decision.* Committee decisions are seldom good quality decisions. To be sure, committee meetings are excellent for marshalling inputs—information, facts, specialized knowledge, attitudes—about a problem situation. But the primary responsibility for a decision should rest with the manager.

· *The notion of expertness.* With increasing complexity and specialization, a manager can seldom rely on his own knowledge and experience alone to reach a decision. He often has to seek expert advice. But this advice should not become a decision. Experts, almost by definition, take a limited view of a situation or problem. Only the manager can maintain a "global" viewpoint.

· *The notion of consultation.* Seeking advice and opinions of colleagues can be useful because of the new perspectives this yields. But it has its dangers. A seemingly convincing argument against a decision can deflect a manager from pursuing it any further. Or, in the other extreme, an overenthusiastic reception can influence a manager to overlook any serious hidden defects that a closer analysis would have detected. Opinions and evaluations from others need careful consideration.

· *The notion of alternatives.* Although the ability to manipulate many alternatives is important, it is even more important to be able to discern the fundamentals in a situation. Effective managers differ from the less effective mainly in their ability to choose and to attend to the more fundamental aspects of a problem. They are able to grasp the heart of the matter, the central point of the problem situation, and cast the superfluous aside.

· *The notion of the unreliability of intuition.* While concrete facts are the building blocks of decision making, the successful manager knows that he can never entirely dispense with a hunch about the situation he faces. There is now considerable evidence that successful decision makers in business rely strongly on their intuitive ability.

· *The notion of automatic acceptance.* Deciding on what to do includes not only what, but also how, when, where, why, and by whom. Most executive decisions have to be implemented by others. This means full cooperation and acceptance of the decision by one's colleagues and subordinates. Yet, as most decision makers know, this is rarely automatic or immediately attainable. A skillful presentation and selling of the decision still lies ahead.

REDUCING THE RISKS OF DECISION MAKING

The basic task for decision making should be a methodical and systematic collecting of information. Only when this work is done can the manager reduce the uncertainty that surrounds the unknown risk and feel that he is adopting a reasonable course. Yet in most organizations the factors of time and cost impose practical limits on the decision-making process. Since with most important situations it is practically impossible to gather all the facts, the manager is faced with these two questions: When does he decide he has *enough* information, and how does he determine that he has the *right* kind of information?

Although no one has come up with any absolute answers to

these questions, there are certain guidelines one can profitably use.

· *Problem definition.* The first task is to define the problem properly. Frequently the apparent problem is not the real source of difficulty at all. It is merely masking or hiding the real problem, which may take some digging to unearth. The manager is well advised to take a hard look at any other facts, rather than the immediately obvious ones, to determine whether he has grasped the heart of the matter.

But accurate problem identification alone is not enough; it also has to be properly stated to enhance the search for a solution. Asking the right questions is an important step toward finding effective answers and solving problems. Questions have considerable power in both opening minds and crystallizing thoughts in the problem solving process.

· *Quantification.* A lot of business information contains numerical data, and many areas permit quantification which may help to clear away the verbal ambiguities and reveal a possible path to a decision. The application of the following three tests to the figures used in arriving at decisions should be helpful:

1. Am I utilizing all the sources of data available to me—from the company, salesmen or suppliers, trade associations, government, business services, trade publications?

2. Is my information up to date, so that sensitive adjustments can be made to slight changes in market, industry, or operations? Information on hand should enable a person to move quickly to avoid trouble or capitalize on opportunities without gambling.

3. How well do I organize and interpret the available figures? A person can gather all the financial and production statistics in existence and still come up with the wrong answers if the relationships between the figures are not clear to him. A manager who is not figure-minded should arm himself with a close associate who can analyze and illuminate the relevant relationships.

· *The cost factor.* Most business decisions fall into two categories: the enhancement of profit or reduction of costs. Gathering relevant information for decisions costs money. The decision maker has to weigh the cost of acquiring information against the money value expected from the decision. For example, a decision about introducing a new product line clearly requires the amassing of much more information than would the layoff of an employee.

· *The time factor.* A decision that is arrived at too late can be as bad as no decision at all. Most business situations are dynamic and constantly changing. A tardy decision usually fails to capitalize on the opportunities presented by change. Even if the action that emerges from a decision is planned for the future, it is better, other things being equal, to make the decision early. Decisions can always be revised in light of further developments, whereas a late decision is usually made in a hurry, which means that inadequate consideration was given to all the factors involved.

· *Stacking the evidence.* The manager should take care not to collect just those data that lead to the conclusion he might favor. Stacking the evidence is a very human failing, but it can be deadly and self-defeating in the decision-making process.

· *The critical factor.* Frequently ideas may look good on paper, until practical considerations are taken into account. These may place severe boundaries or limitations on the alternatives that can be pursued. Practical considerations usually entail factors that cannot be changed because of cost, uncertainty about competitors' reactions, unavailability of certain materials, and so on.

· *Model building.* Most sizable, innovative projects require the building of models to check the theoretical framework. Important business decisions (as, for example, a new sales promotion campaign) require a pilot test before commitment is made to invest huge sums of money. A new idea or a decision of some magnitude should be tried out on a smaller scale before large-scale expenditures and all-out effort are contemplated.

· *Openness to the right experience.* Most managers are bombarded daily with a plethora of stimuli: urgent telephone calls, letters, visitors, meetings, memos, project reports, and many others. As a consequence, one of the most prevalent complaints among managers is that they are too busy to adequately tackle the many decisions they have to make.

Since the quality of decision making depends heavily on the stimuli the manager is exposed to daily, it behooves him to closely examine this massive input. He should appraise the value of each and then make a conscious choice among the various inputs competing for his attention. Improved methods of delegation and staffing would go a long way toward liberating him for a more selective and rational exposure to the stimuli of his environment. This, in turn, will give him better control over, and materially improve, his decision-making ability.

23 | Who's in Charge Here?

1. THE PASSIVE BOSS AND THE PASSIVE SUBORDINATE

This pair might well be characterized as the losers in the corporate world. In an environment where competition is the rule, these people, if they have a friendly relationship, will usually complain about the inconsiderate and blatant "political" behavior of those who are more assertive and aggressive. In their deep sharings of powerlessness they are apt to have lots of ready excuses for things that don't pan out. Most of their suggestions never really get implemented because of their inability to take charge of situations where power-oriented actions are called for. It is much easier for them to bypass resistance problems than to tackle them head-on.

If they are less than friendly with each other, they are apt to complain to their associates about the other's inaction and, if the boss can, he or she will often make the passive subordinate the scapegoat for his or her own limitations on the job. Their relationship with each other is often either alienated and hostile, or fearful and guilt-ridden.

2. THE PASSIVE BOSS AND THE ASSERTIVE SUBORDINATE

This relationship is usually defined by the subordinate who, if a loyal sort of person, will cover up for the boss and accomplish the things the boss should be doing on his own. It is often found in the executive suite that a loyal assertive secretary will, in actuality, carry the load of a weak boss, and be able to prop him up for years by making many of his decisions for him in a subtle way.

If the subordinate is in any way ambitious, he may diligently look for a way to get out of the situation and find a new boss who is more likely to do more for his career aspirations than his current lackluster boss.

3. THE PASSIVE BOSS AND THE AGGRESSIVE SUBORDINATE

This is usually a disastrous combination for the boss, irrespective of whether the subordinate tends to be overt or covert in his or her behavior. If he has no qualms about expressing himself, the subordinate is likely to show open disdain for his boss. He is apt to be angry and testy, and to vocally complain about a great many of the things the boss says or does.

On the other hand, he could be very sly, gossip behind the boss's back, and plant a great deal of doubt about the boss's capabilities in the minds of others, thus undermining what little authority the boss may enjoy because of his position power.

4. THE ASSERTIVE BOSS AND THE PASSIVE SUBORDINATE

If this boss is supportive, has the skills and time, and believes that the subordinate's interpersonal skills can be improved, he may well try to shape up the passive subordinate. On the other hand, he may prefer to assign the subordinate to tasks that better suit the employee's temperamental bent.

5. THE ASSERTIVE BOSS AND THE ASSERTIVE SUBORDINATE

This is usually a very positive combination and there is likely to be a great deal of mutual respect between the two.

Assuming they like each other, this combination is the best of all possible worlds. When the synergistic combination of their interpersonal skills is applied to the resistance of colleagues whose cooperation they need, opposition tends to be overwhelmed in a positive and productive way. These people tend to form a hard-working team that any organization would give its figurative eye teeth to have in abundance, for it is a combination that gets results. Once these two learn how to mesh the nuances of each other's behavior they resonate a kind of teamwork that is seldom developed by even the most astute of management development programs.

Many assertive, creative managers have the flexibility to be cunning and shrewd in the way they handle tactical issues, and plan strategies to get what they want. They can be manipulative, Machiavellian, and quite political, depending on situational demands. They often merely pay lip service to traditional organizational policies, while moving ahead, and accomplishing innovative things.

6. THE ASSERTIVE BOSS AND THE AGGRESSIVE SUBORDINATE

Assuming the assertive boss has the needed skills to control the aggressiveness of the subordinate, this can be a productive, albeit somewhat strained, relationship. The aggressive subordinate must have his or her behavior directed outward to the appropriate targets in the organization, rather than upward toward the boss. Often the behavior of such a subordinate will need to be anticipated and checked, for he is apt to attempt moves to express his restless and often indiscriminating use of power at the expense of others. The boss's biggest task is to keep the subordinate from alienating those in the organization whose support and cooperation they need to accomplish their tasks. If he can maintain control over the subordinate, the energy can be directed in positive ways and productive results achieved.

7. THE AGGRESSIVE BOSS AND THE PASSIVE SUBORDINATE

The aggressive boss usually tends to use the passive subordinate in one of two ways. He may opt for a dependent person or he may simply choose to abuse the person. If these options don't happen to appeal to him, his third choice is to get rid of the subordinate. Such a passive person represents a kind of weakness that he cannot stand. Extremely competitive managers are often at a loss to understand how another person can be so lackadaisical about something as important as winning. To the aggressive manager everything is perceived in black-and-white terms. He ignores things that are not relevant to winning, or he tries to completely conquer those that stand in his way.

8. THE AGGRESSIVE BOSS AND THE ASSERTIVE SUBORDINATE

A suitably assertive subordinate can usually handle an aggressive boss because he knows how to modify the boss's typical win-lose encounter situations to prevent them from escalating into losses for both of them. Often the subordinate will utilize subtle persuasive and palliative devices that look as if he were agreeing with the boss, while at the same time he provides the buffers against possible mistakes. Or he may attempt to bring the boss around to a less aggressive and more palatable point of view.

The assertive subordinate will stand his or her ground in an overt way when the boss becomes too demanding or controlling. Or he may try to find a different position, either within the organization or somewhere else.

9. THE AGGRESSIVE BOSS AND THE AGGRESSIVE SUBORDINATE

This is a mixture a lot like earth and water: it will either make flowers or it'll make mud. If these two happen to get along well, they can be a difficult and formidable combination to work with, for they tend to make life difficult for most of those with whom they interact.

They like to generate, control, and direct conflict and sparks for their own selfish ends and their aggressiveness tends to feed on itself. Many of their meetings with others turn into sessions that conjure up an image of sharks at a feeding frenzy. Rather than try to persuade their opponents, they prefer to chew them up.

If there's little love lost between the two, their relationship is likely to be short-lived, with the boss initiating action to have the subordinate removed. But an aggressive subordinate frequently has ideas of his or her own about who should be the boss, and will not waste any time trying to have the boss removed so he can fill his position.

The power relationship between the executive and subordinate plays a pivotal role in determining how effective the manager can be. Once examined for their basic power patterns, the above combinations can prognosticate whether the boss-subordinate working relationship will be good or poor, and how competitive or cooperative their behavior will be toward each other.

When the relationship between the manager and subordinate is good (e.g., both are assertive), the work progresses well and results are achieved. When the relationship is poor (e.g., boss is passive and subordinate aggressive), difficulties will mount and results are poor.

The perfect or ideal creative manager, as well as subordinate, seems to be the flexible, almost chameleonlike individual who can be alternately either passive, assertive, or aggressive, depending on the situational demands. This individual knows when it is proper to back down, when it is propitious to move ahead with vigor and determination, or when there is no other choice but to thoroughly trounce an opponent so that he cannot, out of revenge, cause harm to him in the future. This type of creative manager is the one who is *really* in charge, and this type of subordinate is, as a rule, eminently promotable.

---

24 | Test Your Work Pattern

SCORING

Add up your points based on the key below.

1.	a.	5	b.	3	c.	0
2.	a.	5	b.	3	c.	0
3.	a.	5	b.	3	c.	0
4.	a.	5	b.	1	c.	3
5.	a.	5	b.	3	c.	1
6.	a.	5	b.	3	c.	0
7.	a.	5	b.	3	c.	0
8.	a.	5	b.	1		
9.	a.	5	b.	3	c.	0
10.	a.	1	b.	3	c.	5
11.	a.	5	b.	1		

12.	a. 5	b. 3	c. 0
13.	a. 5	b. 2	
14.	a. 5	b. 2	
15.	a. 5	b. 3	c. 1
16.	a. 5	b. 3	c. 0
17.	a. 5	b. 3	c. 0
18.	a. 1	b. 4	
19.	a. 1	b. 3	c. 5
20.	a. 1	b. 4	c. 2
21.	a. 2	b. 5	c. 3
22.	a. 5	b. 1	c. 3
23.	a. 5	b. 1	
24.	a. 5	b. 3	c. 0
25.	a. 5	b. 3	c. 1
26.	a. 5	b. 1	
27.	a. 5	b. 1	
28.	a. 2	b. 5	
29.	a. 5	b. 3	c. 1
30.	a. 1	b. 3	c. 4

WHAT YOUR SCORE MEANS

84–147 Your score in this range means your career is of major importance to you and you derive most of your personal identity from it. Such a high involvement may mean that you base too much of your well-being on your career, excluding other important areas of your life you might enjoy. An additional caution is that your exceedingly high commitment may make you susceptible to unacceptable self-imposed stress, and eventual burnout. Managers who endure and succeed in their careers, and sustain their motivation, have many other interests besides their careers. These allow them to develop a more balanced life, and this results in fewer illnesses, healthier relationships, and steadier career achievement.

If you scored very high in this range, you may tend to feel yourself a victim of time pressures and unable to take total control of your time, energy, and life. You surely need to learn to decrease many of the pressures, workloads, and stresses you experience in your work. You also need to explore how you could make your time and energy contribute more to your overall well-being.

57–83 Scores here represent a healthy level of commitment

170

and motivation. To be sure, there might be many things about your work you'd like to change, but, in general, you seem to have found a career that provides you with good psychic income. You've also most likely been able to strike a healthy balance between your work and your personal life.

Although you may feel totally involved in your work, you are not overinvolved, and you relate well to what you are doing and to the people who are working for you. You have a high energy level and can easily marshal extra energy for handling occasional overload situations. You tend not to react to pressure by being driven and aggressive.

24–56 This range indicates that your career commitment is low. This could be due to your being rather dissatisfied with your present job in that it does not match well with your interests and abilities. Or it could be that you tend to be rather laid back, low-key, noncompetitive, and free of any compulsive sense of urgency to better your career.

25 | Do You Fear Success?

SCORING INSTRUCTIONS

To get your score for the test, circle and add up the values for items 1 through 25.

	A	B	C
1.	−1	0	2
2.	2	0	−1
3.	−1	0	1
4.	−1	0	1
5.	1	0	−1
6.	−2	1	2
7.	3	0	−2
8.	−2	1	2

	A	B	C
9.	−1	0	1
10.	2	0	−1
11.	−2	0	2
12.	−2	0	2
13.	−2	1	2
14.	2	1	−1
15.	3	0	−2
16.	2	1	−1
17.	−1	0	1
18.	2	1	−1
19.	3	0	−2
20.	−2	1	2
21.	−1	0	1
22.	−1	0	1
23.	−2	0	2
24.	3	1	−2
25.	−1	0	2

WHAT YOUR SCORE MEANS

28 to 47 You have no problem with fear of success. You are strongly achievement-oriented. You are able to make commitments and persevere with your projects until a successful outcome is assured. You take pride in your creative skills and talents and you have full confidence in yourself. Although independent-minded and assertive, your relationships with others are trustful and open.

4 to 27 You have a tendency to occasionally pursue unrealistically high standards, and you're not always satisfied with your achievements. You prefer win/win rather than win/lose situations. You're concerned about what other managers think of you and you want to be liked by everybody. Because of a fluctuating self-esteem, you periodically lapse into self-critical ruminations about your abilities to succeed. You have some trouble making decisions and then sticking with them. The limelight is certainly not for you, and you regard those who want to be the "life of the party" with scorn. Because you have moderate fear of success, you're not fully using your creative potential.

−25 to 3 You want to win, but frequently lose in the end.

172

You prefer to take the back seat in competitive situations. Because of your excessive need to be liked, you refrain from arguments and contests of will. You lack full self-confidence and you seldom give yourself the credit you deserve for your accomplishments. You tend to be somewhat distrustful of other people's motives and feel that human nature cannot always be relied upon. Fear of success definitely hampers your accomplishments.

−35 to −24 Fear of success is a definite problem for you. You're very nonassertive and consider modesty a virtue. You're never satisfied with your achievements and frequently manage to snatch defeat from victory. Doubtful about whether you've any luck at all, you tend to worry about the future most of the time. Because you're too concerned about others' opinions of you, you frequently act like a "doormat," although you don't like it one whit. You like neither to give nor to receive compliments.

To better understand the dynamics of the fear of success, let's take a look at how it develops.

Most success-fearing managers internalize society's mixed-up attitudes toward success early in life. On the one hand, society extolls the competitive and individualistic spirit. Managers who succeed are admired for their competence, talent, courage, enterprise, and other positive attributes. Those who fail are viewed with contempt or pity. Managers supposedly fail because they are incompetent or lazy. On the other hand, there is a cultural admonition that nice people should be modest, self-effacing, unselfish, and giving. Success is associated with greed and is looked upon as something tacky or even contemptible.

These paradoxical and conflicting attitudes toward success were transmitted to managers through their parents and older siblings. Success-fearing managers were invariably reared in homes where high standards of success and competition were encouraged and valued. At the same time, however, they were discouraged, or even punished, if they were too competitive or if they showed any overt pleasure in winning. The parents of success-fearing managers gave them confusing signals about success and winning, and were highly intrusive in their interactions with them. Many of these parents also expressed strong doubts about their children's abilities to make a mark in the world. In such a home environment, future success-fearing managers learned to perceive others as their rivals who should be defeated. At the same time, they also learned that their competitive drive toward winning frequently

173

evoked the withdrawal of their parents' and their siblings' respect and love. Gradually they learned to control and eventually repress self-assertion and overtly expressed ambition.

Success-fearing managers' early rivalries were filled with feelings of insecurity. They learned to associate winning with unduly depriving, inconveniencing, or hurting others. As these feelings produced a lot of anxiety and guilt feelings, they were driven underground, into the subconscious.

When success-fearing managers grow up, they still retain their ambivalent feelings toward those persons they perceive as rivals. And almost everyone, in one way or another, is regarded by them as a rival. These feelings of rivalry provide them with the initial motivational fuel to defeat their "opponents" and attain the much-envied position of Number One. However, soon after they start to compete, they sense that winning would arouse others' envy and resentment. These feelings, of course, represent a projection of their own suppressed feelings toward the successful. They are in a double bind: failure has to be avoided at all costs because of the humiliation and contempt it evokes, and success is equally unacceptable because then they will become the object of the defeated persons' hostility and envy.

There are at least three clear-cut characteristics that stand out about success-fearing managers.

First, they have a high ambivalence and vacillation about success in that they are initially driven by a compulsive ambition to win, to be first. Then, as soon as they make any significant progress toward attaining success, they get an equally strong compulsion to pull in the reins and to self-sabotage their success. They have a drive both to succeed and not to succeed.

Second, most success-fearing managers cannot justify their behavior rationally because of any experience of negative success consequences in their adult years. There simply haven't been any they can point to. But they continue to maintain their irrational fear of success in spite of any objective evidence to the contrary. The childhood tapes are still being played over and over in their subconscious.

Third, success-fearing managers use a variety of defense mechanisms and rationalizations to protect them from the intense anxiety created both by their initial self-enhancing drives and later self-defeating maneuvers. One of the mechanisms they use is projection of the motives to succeed to external, situational requirements. Another one is a denial of any internal desire to succeed. When, at times, they are successful in spite of themselves, they tend to attribute it to luck, or to others' help, or stupidity, rather than to their own abilities and effort. If this doesn't sound plausible, they tend to say that the accomplishment was easy. By playing down and repudiating their own competence, they manage, in addition, to rob themselves of any real enjoyment of the achievements they do attain.

26 | Letters Will Do

ANSWERS

1. BD   2. DK   3. EZ   4. OK   5. IC
6. IV   7. KT   8. MT   9. NV   10. QT   11. SA
12. SX   13. TP   14. XL   15. XS   16. C
17. LAG   18. XTC   19. IL   20. DR   21. PT
22. SKP

27 | What Does It Mean?

ANSWERS

1. scholarly
2. opinionated
3. undefinable
4. free
5. dilemma
6. contestant
7. waver
8. gibberish

9. adulterate	21. reproach
10. credulous	22. peculiarity
11. confirm	23. intrepid
12. entrap	24. hardy
13. coarse	25. serenity
14. grating	26. swiftly
15. transgress	27. epicure
16. imperative	28. perception
17. temperance	29. negligent
18. obsequious	30. theme
19. belittle	31. trite
20. howling	32. ardent

28 Who Owns the Zebra?

ANSWERS

The Norwegian drinks water; the Japanese owns the zebra.

Houses:	Yellow	Blue	Red	Ivory	Green
Inhabitants:	Norwegian	Ukrainian	Englishman	Spaniard	Japanese
Pets:	Fox	Horse	Snails	Dog	Zebra
Beverages:	Water	Tea	Milk	O.J.	Coffee
Cigarettes:	Kools	Chesterfield	Old Golds	Lucky Strike	Parliament

29 Nitty-Gritty

What is relevant and irrelevant is pretty much a subjective matter. It all depends on your objective for the items listed. Thus, the color of a telephone will be irrelevant if your objective is to improve the telephone's functioning, but it will be very relevant if you are concerned with appearance.

Go back over the attributes you listed and think about why you categorized one attribute relevant and another irrelevant. See if you can learn anything about yourself in terms of the value preferences you have for products. For example, do you tend to value styling over reliability, or do you value both equally?

Another learning aspect of this exercise concerns the number of attributes you listed. How thorough were you when you listed the attributes for each product? Do you think you listed every attribute that could be used to make an improvement? See if there are any attributes you left out. If you tried to visualize the products when doing this exercise you probably didn't list as many attributes as you might have had you looked directly at the product. However, it also may be that some of the attributes you left out were those that you consciously or unconsciously considered to be irrelevant. Again, your value judgments would come into play if this were the case.

---

30 | Stretching Perspectives

Original Objective	Exaggerated Objective	Possible Solution
Economical.	No cost to use.	Solar-powered; will pay for itself in two years.
Fits on desk top.	No desk space wasted.	Recessed into desk.
Produces thirty copies per minute.	Produces fifty copies per minute.	Adjustable copy rate.
Minimal servicing.	Servicing needed every day.	Servicing can be done by user except for six-month checkups.

177

31 | Linear Perspectives

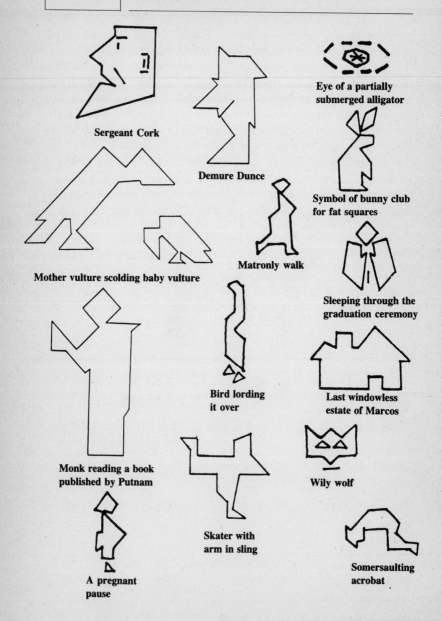

Sergeant Cork

Demure Dunce

Eye of a partially submerged alligator

Symbol of bunny club for fat squares

Mother vulture scolding baby vulture

Matronly walk

Sleeping through the graduation ceremony

Bird lording it over

Last windowless estate of Marcos

Monk reading a book published by Putnam

Skater with arm in sling

Wily wolf

A pregnant pause

Somersaulting acrobat

178

32 | S(i)MILE
When You Say That

POSSIBILITIES

How Is an Iceberg Like a Big Idea?
- It melts with the heat of criticism.
- It floats and moves.
- It can be towed to arid countries.
- It can sink smaller ideas.
- It is slippery.
- It is difficult to come by.
- It grows bigger and gets anchored at the bottom.
- You can chip off chunks to get smaller ideas.
- You'll know it when you see it.
- It doesn't show the work that's gone into it.
- The bigger part is submerged and not obvious to the naked eye.
- It's lonesome—a minority of one.
- It has a commanding presence.
- It gets a cold reception.

How Is a Metal Spring Like Hope?

- It loses its strength after being sat upon often.
- Hope springs eternal.
- It rusts when not in use.
- It gets stiff if not used or acted upon.
- It coils in an upward-spiraling direction.
- It loses its bounciness if sat upon too long or too often.
- If extended way out the coils' shape becomes useless.
- It is wound up with tension.
- It won't let you down.
- It is resilient.

179

- It gives you a goose.
- It renews itself again and again.
- It smooths out the bumps of life.
- It softens the harsh reality.
- It always bounces back.

33 Clustering Ideas

From the list of twenty ideas, the following are representative of the types of groups that might be developed initially:

Grouping	Idea Number
Publications	3, 11, 19
Media	1, 15, 18
Manufacturing	14, 17
Services	7, 13
Solicit funds	4, 5, 8, 10, 16
Sponsor one-time activities	2, 6, 9, 12, 20

These categories then might be combined as follows:

Grouping	Idea Number
Publications	3, 11, 19
Products and services	7, 13, 14, 17
Solicitations and sponsored activities	1, 2, 4, 5, 6, 8, 9, 10, 12, 15, 16, 18, 20

Of course, not all ideas will lend themselves to additional groupings; the decision to do so will depend on the type and number of ideas.

Assuming that some form of categorization is possible, however, the next step is to determine whether any ideas might be combined to produce new solutions. In the example above, the ideas for a telethon, auction, fat cat contributions, and seeking a federal grant could be combined to suggest a new approach. For instance, federal funds might be sought to sponsor a series of monthly educational TV programs that would attract viewers by holding a phone-in auction of items donated by community fat cats. The remainder of the program then would be devoted to discussing educational needs of young children and requesting donations.

34 | What If?

A MANUFACTURER OF SUNTAN LOTION

- Start making vitamin D preparations for sale in the Northern Hemisphere.
- Manufacture makeup for men and women to simulate suntans, and call it "dark-tan" lotion.
- Set up joint venture with lamp manufacturer. He would sell my suntan lotion in the south and I'd sell his sun lamps in the north.

A TOUR ARRANGER FOR A TRAVEL AGENCY

- Give free overcoats to travelers in the north and free bathing suits to southern travelers for booking tours with me . . . a premium to them.
- Offer "zig-zag" tours, across the equator, to see the light and dark sides alternatively.
- Organize aurora borealis tours for Southern Hemisphere inhabitants and South Pole tours for nothern inhabitants.
- Build a hotel in the north, so tall that it catches the sun on its upper floors, and sell "vertical tours" from *darkness* to *light*.

181

ELECTRIC LAMP MANUFACTURER LOCATED IN THE SOUTHERN HEMISPHERE

- Start an air-conditioning business.
- Sell sun lamps in the Northern Hemisphere.
- Start making opaque window shades.
- Buy stock in northern hemisphere power and light companies.
- Invent a "reversible lamp" that can light up dark areas, and darken light areas when it is turned on!
- Sell my good lamps in the north and sell my reject lamps in the south, where no additional light is needed.
- Transfer all my salesmen to North America and Europe.

A ZOO CURATOR IN THE NORTHERN HEMISPHERE

- Build an enclosed Astrodome type of building with controllable daylight-type lighting for the animals.
- Expand the nocturnal animal exhibits.
- Move the zoo to the equator—half of it on the light side and half on the dark side—and shuffle the animals back and forth to maintain their circadian rhythms.
- Send up magnesium flares for eight hours every day to simulate daylight.

---

35 | Verbal Dexterity II

Part One: Jack. Apple. Deal. Egg.

Part Two: Tourmaline. Diamond. Amethyst.

Part Three: Prime. Right. Day. Night. Heart. Fat.

Part Four: AP. GO. PE. OF. AM. AT.

Part Five: Hinder. Honest. Holy.
Harass. Hunt. Hypocrisy. Hypothesis.
Handy. Haphazard. Heroic.

36 Sticky Fingers

The following is presented in a sequential, left-brain manner only to communicate the information more easily. Working through the problem, you will find yourself skipping around quite a bit. However, this disjointed activity will not be too apparent from the description.

GETTING READY

1. I feel very upset that people steal merchandise, since the costs are passed on to the consumer. I also feel upset that some people think they have the "right" to shoplift because of inflation and high prices. On the other hand, I feel sorry for poor people who only take clothes for their children.

2. People shoplift because they are poor, to see if they can get away with it, for the fun of it, because of peer pressure, or because of severe psychological disturbances. Some people have developed elaborate devices (e.g., special boxes with spring doors, coats with pockets sewn on the inside) to aid them; they generally are considered to be professional shoplifters. For other people, the act of shoplifting is more spontaneous. Both employees and customers are guilty of shoplifting. The problem is extremely costly to both stores and customers. Many stores have taken special precautions to thwart shoplifters (e.g., electronic devices, floorwalkers, etc.)

3. I can see someone casually walk through a store, look around, slip a small item into a pocket, and walk out of the store.

4. Expensive merchandise would be displayed more openly; there would be no security measures; prices would be lower; store personnel would observe customers less closely.

5. Whether what I think I know about shoplifting is fact or opinion; how many people in a store at a given time are likely to shoplift something; the type of merchandise stolen most frequently; the type of person most likely to be a shoplifter; the time of day and day of week most shoplifting occurs; the reasons most people shoplift, etc.

6. Discussions with store personnel, consultants, journals, and academic publications.

7. The conditions most likely to tempt someone to shoplift; motives; areas of stores that are most susceptible, etc.

8. Perhaps age of shoplifters and time of day (e.g., teenagers after school hours). Would need to do more research to answer this question.

9. Again, I would need to do more research to answer this question.

10. Teenagers, blue-collar workers, white-collar workers, housewives, people from all economic levels.

11. Coats, sweaters, pants, shirts, blouses, rings, necklaces, tools, etc.

12. In all store departments except furniture and large appliances.

13. At all times of the day; when they think they can get away with it.

14. To save money; to punish themselves; to prove something to someone else; to get back at someone else, etc.

WHAT'S HAPPENING?

1. I can see a lot of people walking around and examining merchandise. There are many different types and sizes of people and a variety of different colors worn by each. I see a lot of glass, metal, and carpeting in the store. There is a constant level of talking, sounds of clothes hangers and necklaces being placed on glass countertops. The glass is very smooth in places, but sticky in other places from constant touching. My feet walk smoothly over the well-worn carpet. I am surrounded by smells of perfume, body odor, leather, and food in a bake shop.

2. The clerk has just turned his head so I probably could slip this tie inside my coat. He just looked in my direction, so I'd better be very careful. Maybe if I just turn my back toward him just a little. There. Now I'll check on the clerk one more time. He's busy now, so . . . oops, here comes another customer, but he's more interested in the suits. Okay, here goes. I'll just pick it up and quickly stuff it in my coat pocket. I won't even look around while I'm doing it. Now, to just casually walk away from here and out of the store. It sure feels good to have gotten away with that. Why did I do that?

3. One positive feature about shoplifting is that it provides a way for some people to obtain merchandise that they couldn't otherwise afford. It also may be a form of psychological release for some people. Other people might benefit from shoplifting by a feeling of social well-being if they deter a shoplifter or report one to store management; it provides an opportunity for people to do a good deed. Stores might benefit from good customer relations by showing customers that management is concerned about the problem and doesn't want to raise prices unnecessarily.

4. Most customers probably aren't very aware that shoplifting is going on unless they happen to observe it directly and the act is very blatant. The shoplifters themselves will be very tuned in to their environment, pick up many visual and auditory cues that other customers might miss. Store employees are likely to be very aware of the actions of customers, especially those who act suspiciously.

5. A lot of loud talking and low lights probably would be attractive to shoplifters.

6. In what ways might shoplifting by customers be reduced? In what ways might store personnel be more aware of potential shoplifters?

LOOSENING UP YOUR MIND

1. A major constraint might be to view a solution as requiring that shoplifters be caught in the act. Another constraint might be to view all shoplifters as alike.

2. Most people may view shoplifters as belonging to the lower economic classes; most people may view shoplifting as not being a major problem.

3. I already challenged these assumptions when I analyzed the problem along other dimensions. I would, however, need to gather data to substantiate my claims.

4. Two taboos would be minding one's own business and not getting involved. Such attitudes would make it much easier to shoplift.

5. Some similar elements would be the need of all shoplifters to avoid being caught, and the fact that most store personnel are trained to watch out for people who may shoplift. Different elements would include such factors as the time of occurrence, the type of merchandise, and the type of shoplifter.

6. Shoplifting is like:

- Taxes—the consumer always pays a price.
- A pack rat—higher consumer prices are exchanged for stolen merchandise.
- Stealing books from a library.
- Cutting grass—the problem can temporarily be eliminated, but always returns.

7. In what ways might customer shoplifting be increased? In what ways might customers be motivated to give merchandise to the stores? In what ways might shoplifters develop a need to turn themselves in?

8.

Original objective	Stretched objective	Possible solutions
Easy to implement.	Difficult to implement.	Frisk all customers as they leave the store.
Increase profits.	Decrease profits.	Give discounts to customers reporting shoplifters.
Maintain good customer relations.	Alienate customers.	Use qualifying standards to enter the store; start a buying club.

9.

Fantasy solution	Practical solution
Read the minds of all customers.	Develop psychological profiles of shoplifters.

186

Fantasy solution	Practical solution
Shoplifted merchandise becomes invisible when taken from store.	Use an exploding dye that is triggered when certain items are removed from a display rack.
A force field prevents shoplifters from entering the store.	Require all coats and packages to be left at the door before entering the store.

10. Nicely ask all customers not to steal anything. A practical solution would be to develop educational programs in the schools and the local news media.

11. In what ways might:

• Customers be screened before entering a store?
• Poor people pay for clothes?
• Shoplifters be less aware of the store environment?
• Merchandise be displayed to reduce shoplifting?
• Subliminal messages be used to discourage shoplifting?
• Store clerks be trained better to detect shoplifting?
• Customers help reduce shoplifting?
• Sounds, lights, textures, colors, or temperature deter shoplifters?
• The public be educated better about the shoplifting problem?
• More shoplifters be caught in the act?
• Shoplifters be encouraged to return stolen merchandise?
• All customers be frisked before leaving a store?

187

(Note: All of these redefinitions of the problem actually are sub-problems that can be used to suggest possible solutions. The major problem is still preventing the occurrence of shoplifting. However, these problem redefinitions help provide a new perspective on the problem. Any one or all of the redefinitions could be selected to use in generating numerous other solutions.)

LETTING GO

1. Offer incentives to return stolen merchandise, establish a bartering unit in each store, increase the number of security personnel, use electronic detection devices, put all merchandise in display cases and order by number, have subliminal messages put in store music, offer discounts to customers reporting shoplifters, convert the store into a buying club with qualifying standards for acceptance, put an electrical field around merchandise that will set off an alarm if tripped, convert to catalog sales, install visible cameras to scan areas of frequent shoplifting, offer free counseling to shoplifters who turn themselves in, stage mock arrests of store employees acting like shoplifters, and have a monthly "shoplifter's day" in which the arrest records of prior shoplifters are made known.

2. Put up a wall, ask them not to do it, physically restrain them, drug them, find out what is rewarding to them and reward them when they don't do it, subject them to peer pressure, lock them in a room, immobilize them, electrically shock them if they try to do it, sit on them, tie them up, educate them regarding the pros and cons involved, glue them down, make a rule, confuse them, and charge them too much money. From these ideas might come such practical solutions as only allowing people to view merchandise without touching it, offering customer discounts if shoplifting is reduced within a certain time period after they have attended an educational program, paying customers to report shoplifters, and selling only very large, expensive types of merchandise.

3. I have selected a glass, a stapler, a telephone, a plant, and a clock. Glass: Put merchandise in display cases, require customers to ask to see merchandise (like asking for a glass of water), use a one-way mirror on the ceiling from which store personnel can watch customers. Stapler: Put merchandise in boxes which require

pushing down on a lever to open. Whenever a lever is pushed down, a light shows on a TV-monitored control station so the customer can be observed inspecting the merchandise, or staple tags to merchandise that must be neutralized electronically before leaving the store. Otherwise, an alarm will sound. Telephone: Call in to store to place orders, then pick up at the store; give customers a constantly changing code number that must be dialed before opening a display case or picking up merchandise to inspect it; pick up merchandise in a store by using a telephone receiver connected to a voice-stress analyzer. Anyone whose voice indicates a high stress level must contact a store clerk for assistance. Plant: Sell only expensive merchandise that customers are not allowed to examine without a clerk; use a photoelectric beam which, if broken, sets off an alarm; or have merchandise rigged so that sound vibrations of it being moved outside of store set off an alarm. Clock: Use a timing device that sets off an alarm hidden in the merchandise unless it is turned off before picking up the object; hypnotize all shoplifters, using a ticking sound, so they'll never steal again.

4. Some of the solutions could be combined as follows: Customers apply for a combination credit card and security card that is used to unlock the store, record who has entered, unlock display cases (recording the card number), and make purchases. Another solution would be to offer discounts to customers who attend educational programs on shoplifting.

BEING DIFFERENT

1. Shoplifting makes me angry because I have to pay higher prices, I have to put up with security devices and suspicious sales personnel, and because some people think they are entitled to steal due to past injustices done to them. Solutions from this "bug" list might include distributing the price increases due to shoplifting among the shoplifters who are caught, and designing a store in which all potential customers would volunteer to undergo a security check so that they would not be bothered by security precautions while in the store.

2. Some possible labels for different solutions would be: Catch-a-Crook; Shopping for Shoplifters (customers turning in shoplifters); The Trading Center, Swap It (for a bartering depart-

189

ment); Big Brother (for store cameras); Crooked Sounds (for voice-stress analyzer); Your Time Is Up (for timed alarm system); Buy-Safe, You're OK (for credit/security card). No new solutions are suggested to me by these labels.

3. Possible solutions from characteristics of a light bulb include:

- Screw-action: secure small appliances with screws; have merchandise rotate in a controlled-access display case.
- Breakable, emits light: to inspect expensive items, a light beam is broken, notifying store personnel.
- Easily turned on and off: a store clerk turns a switch to permit opening a display case for customer inspection of the merchandise inside.
- Filament element: tie down merchandise with a nylon line.

4. It's not easy being a shoplifter. Society looks down on you; you're constantly looking over your shoulder. It's especially awkward at cocktail parties when someone introduces you as their friend the shoplifter. You get very little respect.

If more people realized what was involved in becoming a truly competent shoplifter, perhaps more respect would be given to this elite corps. Considerable planning and organizational skills are needed to pull off a successful "lift"—skills that probably rival those of most business executives. An ability to get along with and relate to other people is essential as well. You must be capable of talking your way out of many difficult situations, and it's always nice if you can relate well to your fellow prisoners and the police. The art of shoplifting has been neglected for too long now, and it is time that more recognition is given to this growing profession. Perhaps what is needed most is development of a professional organization complete with its own public relations department. That and an efficient bail-bonding system would go a long way to upgrading the profession.

Possible solutions suggested by this story are: publication of shoplifter arrest records, formation of a local merchants' committee to combat the problem, and "shock" programs in which first-time shoplifters would visit the local jails and talk with police about the consequences of their actions.

5. Although I am not acquainted with all the measures that have been taken to combat shoplifting, I would guess that some of my solutions are different in the following ways:

- Involving other customers to stem the problem.
- Emphasizing rewards for not shoplifting instead of punishment for doing it.
- Restricting access to a considerable variety of merchandise.
- The notion of a bartering unit to soften the urge to take something from a store.

6. Many of my proposed solutions are modifications of previous solution attempts or solutions currently in practice. For example, many stores keep small, very expensive items in display cases. Some of the solutions use the display case concept, but vary in the way access is gained to the cases.

YOU'RE THE JUDGE

The act of shoplifting, its effect on other people, and the shoplifters themselves may reflect such values as justice, equality, self-esteem, security, power, dignity, and honesty. Any decision as to the best solution should incorporate many of these or similar values.

List of Solutions Generated for the Shoplifting Problem
1. Give discounts to customers reporting shoplifters.
2. Use qualifying standards to enter the store.
3. Convert stores to a buying club.
4. Develop psychological profiles of shoplifters.
5. Use exploding dye on certain items of merchandise.
6. Require checking of coats and packages at store entrance.
7. Use subliminal antishoplifting messages in store music.
8. Train clerks to spot potential shoplifters.
9. Develop public educational programs for the media.
10. Offer incentives for return of stolen merchandise.
11. Establish a bartering unit in each store.
12. Increase the number of security personnel in the stores.
13. Install electronic detection devices.
14. Put all merchandise in controlled-access display cases.
15. Install an electric field around merchandise.
16. Convert stores to catalog sales.
17. Install visible cameras to scan frequent shoplifting areas.
18. Offer free counseling to shoplifters who turn themselves in.

19. Stage mock arrests of store personnel posing as shoplifters.
20. Put on a monthly "Shoplifter's Day" to expose arrest records of prior shoplifters.
21. Offer discounts to participants in shoplifting educational programs if the incidence of shoplifting is reduced.
22. Pay money to customers reporting shoplifters.
23. Sell only large, expensive types of merchandise.
24. Require customers to ask to see merchandise.
25. Install a one-way mirror in the ceiling for store personnel to watch customers.
26. Put merchandise in boxes that require a lever to be pushed to open the boxes; once the lever is pushed, personnel are alerted on a TV monitor.
27. Staple tags onto merchandise; the tags must be electronically neutralized before merchandise can be taken out of the store without sounding an alarm.
28. Assign code numbers to customers to use in opening display cases.
29. Order merchandise in the store by a phone equipped with a voice-stress analyzer; any indication of anxiety requires assistance of a clerk.
30. Merchandise above a certain price requires assistance of a clerk.
31. Install a photoelectric beam above merchandise that sets off an alarm if broken.
32. Use an alarm that is set off by sound vibrations if merchandise is carried out of the store.
33. Use a timing device that sets off an alarm hidden in merchandise if not turned off by a clerk.
34. Hypnotize previous shoplifters so they won't steal again.
35. Use a combination credit/security card to enter store, unlock display cases, and purchase merchandise; require security check to obtain card.
36. Spread any price increases arising from shoplifting among convicted shoplifters.
37. Change store policy so that potential customers must volunteer to undergo a security check to shop without interference of security precautions.
38. Secure small appliances with screws.
39. Have merchandise rotate in a controlled-access display case.

40. Store clerks required to turn switch to open a display case.
41. Tie down merchandise with nylon lines.
42. Form a local merchants' committee to study the problem.
43. Use "shock" probation programs.

Using the numbers of these solutions, I have organized them into five categories, as shown below. (Two of the solutions are listed twice, since they overlap into one other category). Among the solutions that could be easily combined would be: 1 and 22; 4 and 8; 18 and 34; 2, 3, 35, and 37; 13, 27, and 32; 14, 15, 24, 26, 28, 29, 31, 33, 35, 38, 39, 40, and 41; 9, 19, 20, 21, 36, 42, and 43.

Major criteria might include the cost of the effort, its likelihood of success, ease of implementation, effect on customer relations, time required, effect on sales, and extent to which major physical changes in the store would be required.

The criteria could be ranked from highest to lowest importance as follows:

• Likelihood of success.
• Effect on sales.
• Cost.
• Effect on customer relations.
• Time required.
• Physical changes required.
• Ease of implementation.

SCORING INSTRUCTIONS

To compute the score, circle and add up the values assigned to each item.

	OFTEN	SELDOM	NEVER
1.	3	1	0
2.	5	2	0
3.	3	0	0
4.	4	1	0
5.	5	1	0
6.	3	0	0
7.	3	0	0
8.	4	1	0
9.	3	0	0
10.	3	1	0
11.	6	2	0
12.	4	1	0
13.	4	1	0
14.	4	1	0
15.	5	2	0
16.	6	2	0
17.	6	2	0
18.	5	1	0
19.	4	1	0

ANALYSIS

60–76	Extremely poor
40–59	Very poor
20–39	Could stand improvement
0–19	Good

38 Overcoming Managerial Isolation

Part One. Possible steps to improve communication:

· Make yourself accessible. Hear subordinates out and follow through.

· Encourage frankness. Do everything you can to eliminate the fear that speaking up may bring retaliation.

· Welcome new and different ideas. Be willing to listen to all ideas, including those that may seem strange or offbeat. Dismissing offbeat thinking will lead to closed minds and, possibly, the loss of good ideas. Openly reward those whose ideas are accepted. This is the strongest encouragement for further ideas, both from those who are rewarded and from others.

· Listen for the underlying problem. Try to get to what a person is really trying to say. A gripe about working conditions may mask a belief that you don't appreciate his or her job performance.

· Accept criticism. Regard it as healthy and normal. Regard the lack of criticism as dangerous—a sign that subordinates have given up on trying to get through.

Part Two. Examples of directives to issue to reduce isolation:

One way of reducing managerial isolation is to issue a list of "don'ts"; for example:

· Don't try to shield the boss. Many otherwise excellent subordinates think they are doing the boss a favor when they protect him or her from unpleasant news. Instead, by acting as censors, they make him less effective.

· Don't think you have to have the solution before you discuss a problem. Nobody has all the answers, and talking about a problem with your boss can put it into perspective and give both of you fresh ideas.

· Don't expect a problem to disappear if you don't talk about it. This brand of wishful thinking only postpones trouble and compounds the problem.

· Don't overprotect yourself. Occasionally, a subordinate will play down certain facts if he feels they reflect his or her own deficiencies. It is usually impossible to conceal trouble for long, and when it does come to light the boss can think, with some justification, that such a subordinate is less interested in doing a competent job than in saving face.

· Don't dismiss a good idea because it won't affect your operation. If you see a way of improving work methods anywhere in the company, tell your boss about it. Let him take it from there.

SOME THOUGHTS ON THE OPEN-DOOR POLICY

Allowing unlimited access to your office presents difficulties, as anyone who has tried it knows. Also, the telephone seems to be ringing constantly. And schedules must often be rearranged to suit the needs of the moment.

But the inconvenience of the open-door policy is far outweighed by the advantages. You can keep tabs on how the organization is faring through the people you see or talk to. You can settle matters quickly and efficiently on a person-to-person basis rather than through a cumbersome exchange of memos. You can encourage and listen to new ideas that might otherwise never come to your attention.

To avoid being swamped by visitors, you must set up guidelines for what should be taken up with you and what shouldn't. Don't let people use you to make decisions they should be making themselves. Equally important, you cannot let an open-door policy become a door to idle chatter. Learn to define the matter to be discussed, get the facts, discuss the pros and cons, and make the decision. Then end the conversation.

Many managers have found that too many memos and formal meetings leave a barrier between themselves and their subordinates. They prefer to visit a subordinate in his office, where he or she can feel more relaxed.

POSSIBILITIES

1.

This bird suffers from the hardening of alternatives. If anything has been done a certain way for a number of years, he cannot visualize it being done in any other way. This rigid thinking blinderbird can see absolutely no alternative solutions to a problem, no new approaches. If someone attempts to discuss a new solution to an old problem, his words fall hopelessly on deaf ears. He puts on a stony face, acts distant, and uses silence against anyone who feels enthusiastic about a new idea.

2.

This bird is the office Lothario who likes to preen and strut in the presence of females. During ideation sessions, rather than attending to the matter at hand, he is often seen bestowing caresses in endearing tones. Although he claims to be pro creation, his actions show that he is interested more in procreation.

3.

This idea-perforator bird likes to punch holes in every idea not his own. He often jumps to negative conclusions without waiting for the whole story and his call sounds like, "T'won't work, t'won't work!" He is cynical, uses put-downs, and likes to point out only flaws in new ideas.

4.

This very vocal and hard-to-please bird can be downright raucous when anyone deviates from the way *he* thinks a task should be performed. He easily flies off the handle and the atmosphere around him is one of frustration and frenzy. He prefers to feed on nothing but poison ivy berries and others' mistakes which he swells into federal cases before digesting.

5.

This bird is the zipper-lipped idea stopper. The ideas that are passed to him, stop there. He is noncommittal, gives no feedback, and will not express an opinion either pro or con. Since he is so distressingly silent and close-mouthed, his subordinates and associates have the impression that he is not interested in new ideas. He fails to realize that the exchange of ideas and information is what keeps an organization growing and prospering.

40 Problem Situations

POSSIBILITIES

- Encourage employees to identify more with the company and take the company's interests as their own in making work-related decisions.
- Introduce a better fitness program in our company.
- Lessen intergroup conflicts.
- Reduce turnover.
- Make both the extrinsic and intrinsic rewards more effective.
- Eliminate performance deficits.
- Add value to our products in ways different from our competitors.
- Increase participative decision making.
- Counter employees' resistance to setting goals.
- Improve performance evaluations.
- Keep employees fully informed.
- Elicit suggestions for improving overall operations.
- Encourage middle management to delegate more downward.
- Achieve agreed-upon goals more effectively.
- Cut operating costs for our organization.
- Improve efficiency and productivity.
- Improve the morale of our technical professionals.

- Increase secretaries' interest in their work.
- Improve present procedures more effectively.
- Motivate people to achieve desired results.
- Generate more enthusiastic teamwork.
- Help improve the external image of our company.
- Improve people's planning abilities.
- Generate and maintain more enthusiasm in our research and development group.
- Establish and maintain more effective communications.
- Get more creativity out of people.
- Maintain better performance control.
- Get management to set more inspiring examples.
- Increase quality of production.
- Streamline daily routines.
- Reduce accident potential.

Blocks and Barriers

POSSIBILITIES
- Using overly restrictive problem boundaries.
- Oversaturation of familiar sensory inputs.
- Stereotyping.
- Failure to use all the senses in observation.
- Difficulty in seeing remote relationships.
- Narrowing the problem too much.
- Accepting the idea that the problem is beyond one's understanding.
- Failure to investigate the obvious.
- Failure to distinguish between cause and effect.
- Overemphasis on competition or on cooperation.
- Unwillingness to question or to doubt.
- Judging too quickly.
- Fear of criticism.
- Fear of being too aggressive.

- Fear that one's ideas will be stolen.
- Failure to acquire sufficient information.
- An affinity for routine.
- Accepting first solutions that come to mind. Grabbing the first idea.
- Overspecialization.
- Interdepartmental jealousy.
- Poor timing and presentation of ideas.
- Apathy and/or complacency.
- Fear of change.
- Fear of starting something that may backfire.
- Fear of failure.
- Desire to succeed too quickly.
- Low tolerance of ambiguity.
- Failure to incubate.
- Failure to use an appropriate problem-solving language.
- Lack of a questioning attitude.
- Overemphasis on reason and logic.
- Belief that hunches are unreliable.
- Lack of time.
- Environmental distractions.
- Overreliance on experts.
- Pressure for immediate results.
- Inappropriate motivation.
- Incessant effort.
- Concrete or practical-mindedness.
- Intolerance of complexity.
- Habit transfer.
- Lack of interest in problem solving.
- Failure to relate the problem to its environment.
- Inability to see the problem from various viewpoints.
- Inflexible use of problem-solving strategies.
- Inability to abandon an unworkable approach.
- Too much faith in statistics.
- Fear of asking questions that show ignorance.
- Undue concern with the opinion of others.
- Excessive involvement with others and neglect of own needs.
- Fear of being a pioneer or first in a field.
- Attitude of playing it safe.
- Lack of initiative or self-starting ability.

- Lack of spontaneity—inability to let capacities flow of themselves.
- Poor physiological and psychological health—illness, tension, pain, anxiety, and so forth.
- Lack of appreciation of the value of imagination, fantasy, humor, dreaming; inability to open-mindedly tune in to messages from within.
- Failure of management to recognize and reward creative ability.
- Autocratic boss who values only his or her own ideas.
- Lack of long-range objectives.
- General distrust of originality.
- Emphasis on immediate functional utility of ideas.
- Tendency of management to tell the creative person what to do and how to do it.
- Frequent changes of key decisions.
- Lack of effective communication between employers and management.
- Poor handling or outright misappropriation of credit.
- Problems of creative work settled by fiat from above.
- Creativity—within limits.
- Overemphasis on teamwork.
- Management's tendency to look at a proposal with one question in mind: "What's wrong with it?"
- Management's attitudes: "It was good enough ten years ago, it's good enough now," or "We are not going to take any chances."
- Inflexible work schedules.
- Lack of cooperation and trust among colleagues.
- Competition with "promoter-type" colleagues.
- Lack of appreciation and recognition by management of creative contributions.
- Tight project management.
- Lack of understanding of the really creative person and his or her motivation.
- Too many hack assignments.
- Too many inaccurate schedules.
- Lack of authority to match responsibility.
- Too many deadline crises.
- Lack of participation in the selection of projects.

42 | Managing Creative People

ESSENTIALS:

Tact and insight: To maintain a favorable daily climate, a manager of creative people has to have tact, good judgment, and insight into diverse personalities. A staff of creative people probably represents a greater diversity of temperament than does a similar-sized group of almost any other type of white-collar specialists. Intensifying the problem, creative people probably experience wider and more frequent fluctuations in individual mood.

Respect for individual differences: One of the most important traits of the creative manager of people is the ability to handle diverse personalities. He must recognize, for example, that some creative people work best when given considerable freedom, while others need guidance and structure. The manager analyzes the motives of each person separately and then tries to develop each in the most suitable direction. Conflicts arise when the creative person has one self-image and perception of his or her role and responsibilities, and the manager another. The creative manager tries to bring these images into clearer focus.

Understanding of creative problem solving: The creative manager understands the difficulties implicit in the creative process. He knows that the flow of ideas is more likely to be pulsating than continuous, and also knows that a period of sterility does not always mean that the potential has dried up, but rather that new strength and direction are being gathered.

The creative manager also has insight into the things that inhibit creativity and knows that limited creative output is frequently due not to lack of creative ability, but to inner blocks and barriers. He has mastered some of the methods which can be used to overcome these inner blocks.

Professional competence: While not as up to date in every detail of their activities as are the creative staff, the creative manager nevertheless has the knowledge to discuss their problems at any point of a project's development. Without this background of

203

fundamental knowledge, the manager cannot adequately communicate with each member of the staff and win the necessary respect and confidence. Studies have shown that a lack of respect for one's superior is the greatest cause of employee dissatisfaction.

Ability to communicate: Skill in communicating spans such areas as the ability to express ideas clearly, the ability to lead and arbitrate discussions, and the ability to ask intelligent, searching questions that stimulate, spur, and encourage thinking and problem-solving. The creative manager has also mastered the skills of listening, not only to what is said, but to what lies behind the words.

Sense of security: The creative manager must want to see subordinates succeed without being afraid or envious of them. Such a manager should understand his own motivations too, and be conscious of his own attitudes and prejudices. Awareness of one's own negative attitudes enables one to inhibit their expression and forestall any reinforcement of the negative attitudes of subordinates.

The creative manager leans over backwards to see that the group gets credit for accomplishments. This manager never dominates the group and produces ideas without showing off. He is accepted by the creative people more as a colleague who is respected than a boss who has a position of authority.

Ability to assign responsibility: The creative manager makes assignments that conform to the personalities, interests, and abilities of subordinates. To do this, he spends a great deal of time finding out what the particular strengths and weaknesses of the people are, and what interests them most. The manager then tries to assign each person to a task or project in which each can take an active interest, find satisfaction, and find greatest chances for contribution. The highest kind of creativity can only emerge when the individual feels a personal affinity for an area of interest.

Ability to criticize tactfully: The creative manager is able to suspend critical judgment in the beginning stages of a project. It bears emphasis that nothing can inhibit creativity more than critical evaluation applied prematurely. Judgment, evaluation, and criticism have their place, but only at the conclusion and at the beginning or middle of a creative venture.

Ability to provide inspiration: Creativity thrives on encouragement and inspiration. The creative manager needs plenty of contagious enthusiasm. He must provide the inspirational beginning for a creative undertaking and show faith that the staff will be able to successfully solve the problems. While the project is under way, the manager continues to show active interest and readily recognizes the progress made. He provides the necessary moral support during the difficult stages of the project.

Receptiveness: The creative manager convinces the members of the group that all ideas will be considered and that people will be properly identified with their parts in successfully solving problems. Ideally, a formal system should exist for the fair and consistent consideration of all ideas conceived in a department. In any case, the manager considers all new ideas and rewards successful efforts immediately.

Knowledge of when to take an idea: The effective manager knows when to take the idea from the creative person. He knows that if it is taken away too soon, resentment results and further development of the idea might be hindered. The manager is also aware that if he does not take the ideas after they have been completed, the creative person might see this as evidence of neglect or rejection, not only of the ideas but of himself or herself.

Ability to bolster self-confidence: Self-confidence plays a tremendous role in creativity. Fear of criticism, fear of a manager's or colleagues' opinion or disapproval, doubts about one's own ability, fear of appearing too revolutionary or unusual—all of these feelings, or any one of them, can inhibit or suppress creativity.

Although the manager's optimism should be tempered with realistic considerations, at the initial stages of creative work it would benefit greatly if he is more optimistically inclined. Therefore, a basic optimism and a stubborn refusal to give up, no matter how great the difficulties initially encountered, are two important qualities in the creative manager's personality makeup.

Insistence on flexible organization: The creative manager knows that many of the standard principles, methods of organization, and patterns of management are not applicable to creative work and creative people without considerable modification. He is aware of the requirements for flexibility in the department and knows that these preclude the rigid design that can be applied to most other functions in the organization. Consequently, rather than trying to fit the creative people into a predetermined organizational structure, the creative manager helps to mold the structure to fit the individuals.

43 | Teamwork Dynamics

PART ONE POSSIBILITIES

Increased efficiency: Because team members give primacy to common rather than individual goals, efforts count for more and resources are not wasted on peripheral or unnecessary activities.

Heightened motivation: For most subordinates, being a member of a team produces a sense of belonging and acceptance that has a powerful effect on motivation. A subordinate who feels a close identification with members of his team will want to maintain that rewarding relationship. If the team is goal oriented, each individual will act in accordance with the expectation of high performance.

Improved quality control: Members of an effective team take pride in their performance. They do not tolerate shoddy work, because this reflects badly on the entire group. Thus, there is a built-in quality-control mechanism. In the right organizational climate, team members will set standards that are higher than those imposed by their manager.

More flexible operations: An effective team has members who can wear several hats. Since no one is indispensable, important activities are not paralyzed when individuals are absent.

Enhanced creativity: Teamwork provides for the cross-fertilization of ideas that is imperative for creative results. The number of catalyzing stimuli that can spark a new idea is greater in a group than what an individual can get when working alone. Teamwork stimulates discussion, fosters the pooling of knowledge, and exposes a person to many different viewpoints and facets of a situation.

Mutual support: The members of a successful team support one another, especially when one of them runs into difficulty. They are also receptive to suggestions and criticisms from within their own ranks, provided the relationships between members are open and noncompetitive.

PART TWO POSSIBILITIES

- Manager's ability to create and sustain a spirit of enthusiasm and cooperation.
- His ability to create an atmosphere in which the team spirit evolves naturally, and not coercively.
- His ability to enhance cooperation and willingness to show that he has confidence in his team.
- The manager should be tuned to the effects that staff members have on one another. Group cohesiveness is fostered when there is mutual respect. This does not imply that all team members must like one another—only that everyone should be open and tolerant. Teamwork is a complex phenomenon. It depends on working relationships in which responsibility, innovation, and disagreement are encouraged. There has to be a high tolerance for differences in personalities and opinions.
- Convincing the team that cooperative action serves a purpose that is beyond the reach of their independent contributions.
- Clear definition of a common challenging purpose.
- Full participation in the decision-making process and in planning of group's activities.
- Breaking down the purpose into short-range goals and long-range objectives, with signposts established to indicate progress toward goals and objectives.
- Building of mutual loyalty by holding frequent meetings, openly discussing problems, and encouraging team members to come up with suggestions on how to solve problems.
- Maintaining open and nondefensive communication among team members.
- Sharing of information and progress reports.
- Nipping any conflicts, jealousies, feuds, and self-centered behavior at the bud.
- Maintaining a posture of fairness by encouraging team members to speak out about problems and issues that affect the performance of the entire group.
- Fostering a climate of trust, enthusiasm, and collaboration.
- Awareness of any underlying animosities that could have a negative impact on teamwork.

Dealing with recalcitrants: One of the manager's toughest problems is to change the attitudes and behavior of a subordinate who has become apathetic. Often, an increase in responsibility, new or better assignments, and eyeball-to-eyeball confrontations can turn such a person into a useful team player.

Another recalcitrant is the loner, who prefers to work by himself. If he is productive, it would be useless to radically change his style of working. However, putting him into a job-rotation program or giving him the role of "resource specialist" might evoke in him more of a sense of identification with the team.

A subordinate whose work and ideas have been frequently criticized or rejected may withdraw to one degree or another from group participation. One way of bringing him back to the team is to give him encouragement and help when he starts a new project. He also needs plenty of praise for his contributions; especially when he overcomes difficulties by his own efforts.

Another individual who works outside the team orbit is the one who is overly ambitious and competitive, particularly where promotions are concerned. He regards associates in the group as rivals, not team members. The manager can rechannel his egocentric drives somewhat by rewarding his efforts only when he cooperates with others.

44 Closed/Open Systems

If your ratings fell on the upper ends of the scales (5–10), the present climate of your organization or department is already conducive to creative behavior.

Both systems are, in a sense, cyclical and continuous. The open system results in a creative growth cycle, which meets the human needs necessary and fundamental for learning, creativity, and psychological health; the closed system results in a vicious cycle of restriction, suppression, and loss of creativity.

45 How to Evaluate Ideas

The following idea evaluation checklist, developed by Princeton Creative Research, can help you formulate one that would be suited to your requirements.

1. Is the idea simple or complicated? Can people understand it without lengthy explanation?
2. Could you work out several variations of the idea, to afford those who will judge it a freedom of choice? Could you offer alternate ideas?
3. Will it work in actual practice? Is it feasible?
4. Have you checked the idea for any possible faults or limitations?
5. Have you pinpointed the exact problem situation or difficulty your idea is expected to solve?
6. Are there any problems the idea might create? What are the changes involved?
7. What immediate or short-range gains or results can be anticipated? Are the projected returns adequate? Are the risk factors acceptable?
8. What long-range benefits can be anticipated? Will they support company objectives?
9. Have you checked the operational soundness of the idea? Can it be made by the company? Are company's engineering, production, sales, distribution facilities adequate for implementation?
10. How well does it fit into the current operation of the organization?
11. Can the company afford it? Have you considered the economic factors of its implementation—what person/talent, time for development, investment, marketing costs, etc., does it entail? What personnel will be involved? Who else is needed to perform the job?
12. How simple or complex will its execution or implementation be?

13. Is there a real need for it? Does it have a natural sales appeal? How ready is the market for it? Can customers afford it? Will customers buy it? How timely is the idea?
14. What, if anything, is competition doing in this area? Can your company be competitive?
15. Have you considered the possible user resistances or difficulties?
16. Does your idea fill a real need or does the need have to be created through promotional and advertising efforts?
17. Is it compatible with other products or services of the company and its overall objectives?
18. Are there any specific circumstances in your organization that might make the acceptance of the idea easy?
19. Are there any specific circumstances in your organization that might make the acceptance of the idea difficult?
20. How soon could it be put into operation?

From this self-questioning checklist a device can be constructed that would be useful in evaluating ideas concerning almost any other type of organizational problem.

For example, a cost-reduction objective would entail an analysis of actual present and projected costs, the "reason-whys" for these costs, areas where the opportunities for cost reduction exist, and what is known about present methods and procedures.

A problem involving production would have to take into account the existing facts about the actual production operations, the repertoire of the worker skills involved, available equipment, plant layout, together with what would be needed for a more desirable situation.

If the problem involves management or supervisory training, the factors would be found in an analysis of company's objectives, present performance of management personnel, and the areas where improvement is sought.

One important but often overlooked point when evaluating ideas is to consider whether the changes the idea will bring about are desirable or undesirable regarding the people who will be affected. What real benefit will accrue to the people involved? Will it be perceived as fair to all? Ideas that call for radical changes in procedures, organization, duties, or responsibilities particularly deserve a great deal of thought. Neglecting to consider the payoffs and benefits and how people will be affected has caused many potentially promising ideas to fail.

46 | The Politics of Selling Ideas

SCORING

For each item allow two points if your answer was right, zero if it was wrong. Then total your score and read the interpretation to see how it represents your political ability to sell ideas.

1. True	16. True
2. True	17. False
3. False	18. True
4. False	19. False
5. False	20. True
6. False	21. True
7. True	22. True
8. False	23. False
9. False	24. True
10. False	25. True
11. False	26. False
12. True	27. True
13. True	28. False
14. True	29. True
15. False	30. False

INTERPRETATION

Your score gives you a general idea of your overall ability to handle the political/power issues involved in selling your ideas to decision makers. The higher the score the more aggressive and political you are. A low score, on the other hand, indicates that you have a reluctance to maneuver on your own behalf.

Your score places you on a continuum ranging from passive/nonpolitcal on one extreme to assertive/active in the middle to aggressive/political on the other extreme:

Passive/Nonpolitical	Assertive/Active	Aggressive/Political
0 10 20	30 40	50 60

A person falling at 14 or below on this scale is almost certain to have a very difficult, if not impossible, time in pressing his or her own cause. Of course, being assertive is no guarantee of success either, since many aggressive people can block ideas. One must be prepared to handle them with some specially honed assertive skills or the odds are that they will win. Then too, two aggressive rivals can do a pretty good job of chewing each other up.

The best combination appears to be a mixture of assertive skills with a dollop of aggressiveness to back you up when needed. In general, however, assertive skills, when used with tact and insight, are sufficient for idea-selling situations.

Persuasiveness is not a linear correlation with the passive/assertive/aggressive dimension. It is curvilinear.

Extremely Political and Aggressive: A score of 46 or more classifies you as very politically oriented. You have the drive to push your ideas, but your big problem might be the resistance and the enemies you create in the process. Anyone who is so strongly power-oriented cannot help but show it in one way or another, and people are apt to resent raw manifestation of ambition. If your style is to use unvarnished power consistently and without letup, eventually even the most passive members of your organization will join forces and challenge you. The tactical and strategic losses you sustain, as a result, could make your future idea-selling a flash in the pan.

Assertive/Active: The mid-range of scores between 14 and 46 show a skill level for representing yourself in an effective and persuasive manner. You are probably astute enough to identify opportunities to present your ideas with a good sense of timing for audience readiness. You are also likely to be flexible enough to sense when to be shrewd and careful, and when to be open and direct. One of the effective talents of the mid-range scorer is his or her ability to recognize when to withdraw and when to press events to closure and action. An assertive person is usually aware of the efficacy of power and politics, but he is selective in its use rather than being driven by it, or afraid of it.

Passive/Nonpolitical: The lower-range, 0–14 scorer is usually a passive person—frequently a mild-mannered idealist—who is prone to keep his nose entirely to the grindstone and to be oblivious to the political aspects of selling ideas. Rather than develop and cultivate contacts with key people, this person expects to receive recognition automatically for his ideas. Unfortunately, the psychology of visibility requires direct action on behalf of one's ideas. Recognition and acceptance of ideas do not happen on the basis of a subjective notion of what is "fair" or meritorious.

A low-scoring person is often the one who has good ideas, but is his own worst enemy when it comes to selling them. This person definitely needs "allies" to get his ideas across.

Estimating your chances for success in idea selling should be based on an evaluation of several issues:

- The appeal of your idea to the key decision makers.
- The degree of ease or difficulty you will have in achieving support and consensus on your idea from key decision makers.
- Your ability to overcome the inertia, customs, practices, and resistance within your organization.
- The effectiveness of your idea in solving the perceived pressing needs of the organization.

The simplest way to estimate your chances of success is to conduct a series of interviews with key executives whose jobs will be affected by your actions. Select those who are in key posts on the organization's chart—the higher up, the better.

If your idea is likely to be perceived as causing interference in the work of these key people, you can obviously expect evasiveness, partial truths, or devious subterfuges. You can, however, piece together the fragments of a dozen or so interviews and begin to see the drift of the potential obstacles, existing rivalries and possible points of agreement. You may be able to utilize that information to reach an eventual consensus.

The interviews serve the dual purpose of providing information about the situations you must tackle as well as giving you means to present yourself as *nonthreatening*. You should try to delay any incipient resistance as long as possible to give you time to develop your plan.

Obviously, at this stage you will want to keep your cards close to your vest in order not to give anyone a chance to build effective barriers even before you get started. This means taking a neutral, fact-finding stance. You should not, at this point, advocate any specific attitude or position that would prematurely give away your plan.

ASSESSING YOUR SITUATION

To estimate your chances of success you need answers to the following questions:

· What are my assets and strengths? What are my weaknesses and liabilities?

· Who will be my major allies? Whose interests and needs will be served by my efforts? Who will be my rivals, opponents, or resisters? What are their particular strengths and weaknesses?

· Who belongs to various cliques and coalitions? Who is perceived as my sponsor or "godfather"? How will I best be able to form a power base? Through know-how? Connections? Reputation?

· What are the organizational mechanisms used to make decisions? Habit? Committees? Budgeting processes? Momentum? How can I use or change institutionalized decision-making patterns to my advantage?

· Can I get the resources needed for an effective effort?

· How far will my boss and allies extend themselves before I reach the limits of their risk-taking ability and self-interests?

· Is there any issue with sufficient visibility and impact that I can use for leverage?

· Is the timing or organizational situation right for my idea, or could it smother my plan?

· Can I use external pressures or events for leverage, such as media coverage, economic changes, legislative events, or industry associations?

There may be, of course, other considerations, but these are the basic ones that will provide an estimate of the odds in your favor.

Since no one person's perspective is foolproof, it is very important to consider getting someone qualified to help you think through the answers to these questions.

SUCCESS FACTORS IN SELLING

Success in launching a new idea or program depends to a large degree on a combination of one's political acumen and managerial reputation. The political aspects of the plan require a sensitivity to what others want individually and in the aggregate, and how that translates into the program that you want to implement.

As a rule, it is helpful to be effective at socializing. It is the lubrication for the machinery of power in the organization. It lowers the instinctive barriers erected to "outsiders," whether it be across divisional or professional boundaries, or whatever way turf is defined in the organization's status and in-group mechanisms.

An instinct for leverage is a primary success factor. The program that you want to launch must serve the needs of the organization, and especially the needs of those individuals who are influential in the organization's most important processes and decisions. The program or idea that you plan to launch and the issues that you tackle must produce a large yield for your effort. Conserve your energies for doing only those things that can be effectively implemented and that have a high visibility. Here the 80–20 rule applies: Eighty percent of the results will come from 20 percent of the effort. A searching analysis must be done to identify the 20 percent that will provide the leverage and odds in favor of success and then apply 100 percent of the effort to those issues, concerns, or problems.

The creative manager must be *seen* as competent. In this sense, selling the sizzle is at least as important as selling the steak. This is not a recommendation to be deceptive but simply a recognition of the fact that human perceptions are not objective, but are, rather, a function of subjective needs of the audience. Trying to change belief systems, trying to make converts with evangelistic fervor, or pushing a personal point of view are counterproductive. The bottom line cannot be reached without managing the party line appropriately.

You need to develop a campaign theme that is easily recognized and clearly identified with you and your idea. The theme, or rallying idea, can act like a magnet and eventually draw many other ideas and follow-on programs to it. Themes that have been used successfully in the past have common denominators that should be exploited, such as productivity, profits, innovations, new technology, diversification, work simplification, and many more.

The creative manager must be dominant. He must be willing to persist in the face of setbacks and put on an aggressive campaign for his program. Waffling on the program's goals invites defeat, although reworking and other secondary compromises can be expected. Dominance does not necessarily mean being right, but being effective and achieving the objective that is set. It is important to remember that there are many ways with which the issues and problems can be solved, and there is no sure way to know, or to prove in advance that one way is better than another in any absolute sense. There is considerable wisdom in the saying that an ego trip that insists on personal preferences which allow no compromise is a short trip indeed. Therefore, the strategic innovative manager must find the issues that can be solved with different combinations, so that no single point of resistance can stop progress, but serves, instead, as a cue for recombining the resources of tactical logic, to get around the problem.

Finally, success depends on not spreading one's efforts too thin. It is wise to stick to one or two essentials that can be delivered with impact. Concentrate the firepower in focused efforts.

FACT-FINDING SOURCES

To increase your chances of success, there are numerous sources of information that are often overlooked:

· Your peers at other companies can not only provide you with ideas for your own efforts but cite impressive examples that you can use to bolster your own arguments in presentations. A typical question that a new idea frequently elicits is: "Who else is doing it now?" Imitation is the sincerest form of anxiety reduction. If someone else has done it and it works, others feel safe in trying it.

· Other managers can be useful resources but they are not always reliable because of their own self-interests and hidden agendas.

· Business and technical magazines are invaluable for providing ideas that have survived peer scrutiny to be published. Quoting from relevant published materials can add power to your persuasiveness.

· Consultants are routinely employed these days. They provide an excellent perspective in planning your key moves as well as being on call to assist in implementation.

· Company publications are too often shunned because of the time it takes to wade through the reading. Although less interesting and direct than asking old-timers about what has been going on, there is a message in the way the official "packaging" presents the company image. It speaks volumes about the organization's climate and culture. Especially important are the things *not* discussed, the taboos.

After assessing yourself and the situation to sort out your chances, analyze what you have found, test your conclusions and feelings, then take the plunge. There is no room for timid attempts at success.

47 | Implementation

AN OUTLINE FOR THE IMPLEMENTATION OF AN APPROVED IDEA.

1. *Assign a project manager.* The assignment of a manager is essential to the successful implementation of the proposal.
2. *Acquire operating funds.* One of the initial actions taken by the project manager is to confirm the project status and arrange for the operating funds to be assigned to the project.
3. *Form an implementation staff.* The implementation staff should consist of representatives from the departments directly involved with the implementation actions of the project.
4. *Reconfirm the milestone plan.* As part of the preparation for presentation, a milestone plan is developed identifying major events. These milestones are go/no-go gates designed to reduce the investment risk. The plan may also recommend the parallel development of one or more alternative approaches. The parallel development provides a backup plan in the event a problem is encountered that requires a major shift away from the primary approach. Since it is part of the original approved plan, these changes in direction can be made without disrupting or requalifying the entire plan.
5. *Develop and test.* All elements of the proposal that can be tested and verified prior to incorporating should be completed and well documented. Some proposals, such as procedure changes, may not be easily tested prior to

217

implementing. The effects of these changes, during implementation, need to be observed and documented for early
signs of problems.
6. *Report progress.* Progress reports should be presented to
the decision makers at regularly scheduled meetings and
when a major milestone is completed.

The following are guidelines for progress reporting:
   a. Submit agenda and documentation before meeting.
   b. Identify milestone completions and all open issues.
   c. Report expenditures against budget.
   d. Present recommendations and corrective actions.
   e. Report probabililty of success confidence level.
   f. Open discussion.
   g. Schedule next meeting.

The manager should follow the progress of the project to
obtain feedback on the implementation plans and on the cost estimates generated by the study team. Any significant discrepancies
between the estimated and actual costs, any unanticipated technical problems, or any implementation problems should be cri-
tiqued by the study team to improve their performance. A
continuing acceptance of a problem-solving effort will depend on
the quality of output. A constant monitoring of the actual results
will assist the problem solver in maintaining a quality output.

48 Innoways

POSSIBILITIES

• Have each issue feature articles by recognized creative individuals in a variety of occupations and professions.
• Feature a column, "Creative Forum," where innovative

ideas would be suggested by readers on how to solve everyday problems.
- Notable and fascinating "firsts"—breakthroughs in any field or area.
- Solicit ideas from readers starting a new business and feature those regularly.
- Creative games, exercises, and puzzles for readers to solve.
- Feature articles on new creative problem-solving methods and techniques.
- Reviews of books dealing with creativity.
- Case histories of successful creative problem solving in business and industry.
- Articles based on interviews with creative people.
- Feature regular "What Would I Have Done" problems for readers to solve.
- Articles on how ideas became huge success stories (e.g., Xerox, Polaroid, videotape, computers, etc.).
- Articles on how leisure time can be used creatively.
- Memorable quotes on creativity by famous creative people.
- Review of best creative ads and TV commercials.
- Explanation of concepts and techniques useful in creative problem solving.
- Descriptions of new and notable patents issued.
- Stories on how creative thinking enabled a person to overcome an emotional or physical handicap.
- Periodic contests of best ideas contributed by readers to solve a specific problem.
- Review and critique of articles by creativity researchers.
- Start a "Creativity Book of the Month Club."
- Describe ideas and products that were developed by utilizing specific creative problem solving techniques.
- Stories on how human relations, civic, and community problems were solved creatively.
- Run articles that emphasize the fun aspects of creative problem solving.
- Feature articles on how anyone can increase his or her creative ability and output.
- Articles on how creativity contributes to the enjoyment of living.

49 20/10 Vision

POSSIBILITIES

- Robots are widely available to help clean house, prepare meals, do other domestic chores.
- There is radical reduction of cost in buildings for home and business.
- Pollution will be reduced without impairment of comfort or nation's economic health.
- Due to artificial surfaces and inexpensive construction of ski slopes in flat country, skiing will become a year-round sport.
- Recreation lands are getting scarce. Government provides incentives to make private lands public.
- Over half of payroll costs go toward benefits, including insurance.
- More people conduct business from home.
- Over 60 percent of American wives have jobs.
- World population will top 7.5 billion.
- Farmers will be able to get twice as many crops from the same acreage.
- Living quarters can be quickly and inexpensively rearranged to suit changing needs.
- Grocery and department stores will be fully automated.
- More indoor recreation centers will simulate outdoor environments.
- Most people live in urban areas, which comprise a full third of the United States.
- Structures will be designed to accommodate both residential and business use, to conserve space and eliminate commuting.
- There will be new materials for heating and cooling.
- Automated banking, credit, and audit systems are in universal use.
- Computers widespread in translation, teaching, libraries, traffic control, crime detection, design and analysis.

- The United States has put mandatory population control into effect.
- Manmade islands are constructed for recreational use.
- Increasing leisure contributes to mental illness.
- The average retirement age is forty-six.
- Translating machines are commonplace.
- Widespread facsimile systems, telephone pictures, and print.
- Supersonic aircraft fly 2,000 miles an hour.
- Computers and automation operate in all areas of management and production.
- New sources of power in the form of storage batteries, fuel cells, electromagnetic fields are available for ground transportation.
- International seminars are conducted through television and commercial satellites.
- Automated highways and moving sidewalks will be introduced.
- Life expectancy for American reaches 85 years.
- Effective control of aging through dietary, hormonal, and cultural factors.
- Eighty percent of cancers will be controllable.
- Electrical control of pain will be widespread. Suspended animation will be used in medical treatment.
- New rejuvenation techniques will be introduced.
- Vaccine will be developed to conquer the common cold.
- It will be possible to choose the sex of unborn children.
- Health will be monitored at home with computers and interactive cable TV.
- The first human clone is created.
- There will be chemicals and drugs to treat depression, psychoses, and neuroses.
- Nuclear wastes will be dumped in space by automated spacecraft.
- A satellite system provides solar power from space.
- The United States has a shortage of drinking water.
- Controlled underground nuclear explosions produce natural gas and oil.
- Two-week weather forecasts will be reliable.
- Earthquakes will be predictable up to a month ahead through satellite systems.

221

- There will be large-scale ocean farming.
- A computer scores above 160 on a standard IQ test.
- Chemicals and drugs improve memory, learning, and intelligence.
- Several international terrorist groups will have nuclear weapons.
- Effective terminal defense by directed energy beams has been developed.
- There is some colonizing of planets and a permanent lunar installation.
- There will be permanent inhabited undersea installations and colonies.

50 Never Reject an Idea . . .

INJUNCTIONS

- Never reject an idea because it's impossible.
- Never reject an idea because your mind is already made up.
- Never reject an idea because you don't have the money, manpower, muscle, or months to achieve it.
- Never reject an idea because it will create a conflict.
- Never reject an idea because it's not your way of doing things.
- Never reject an idea because it might fail.
- Never reject an idea because others who tried to make it work, failed.
- Never reject an idea because it is merely a hunch and you don't have the data to back it up.
- Never reject an idea because it was previously rejected.
- Never reject an idea because it seems ambiguous, or far-fetched.
- Never reject an idea because you don't understand it.